HARVARD MIDDLE EASTERN MONOGRAPHS

IV

PAN-ARABISM AND LABOR

BY

WILLARD A. BELING

DISTRIBUTED FOR THE
CENTER FOR MIDDLE EASTERN STUDIES
OF HARVARD UNIVERSITY BY
HARVARD UNIVERSITY PRESS
CAMBRIDGE, MASSACHUSETTS
1961

Second Printing, 1961

LIBRARY OF CONGRESS CATALOG CARD NUMBER 60–15082

PRINTED IN THE UNITED STATES OF AMERICA

PREFACE

Broadly speaking, pan-Arabism represents a conscious effort to create a united Arab Nation whose antecedents are sought in early Islamic history. To be sure, this history and a common religious heritage also embrace Turkey, Iran, Pakistan, and other Islamic states. Nevertheless, by virtue of their non-Arabic languages and other differences they are normally excluded from the pan-Arab concept, albeit not from a related pan-Islamic dream. This study concerns only the Arab states, from Morocco to the Persian Gulf.

In recent years, Egypt has assumed active leadership of the pan-Arab movement. The successful revolution in Egypt had, among other things, demonstrated the potential of directed mass movements. Therefore, by various means she sought to create a similar broad popular base for pan-Arabism in the working classes of the Arab world. And in a real sense, the pan-Arab labor movement is a reflex of Egyptian-sparked Arab nationalism. This study then, quite correctly, first examines the movement to determine whether it is a bona fide labor movement or merely a political vehicle.

In any case, the pan-Arab labor movement has touched national labor movements throughout the Arab world, with varying reactions. As for the international labor organizations, the very fact that the pan-Arab labor movement follows a course of "positive neutrality" immediately made it suspect in the eyes of the anti-Communist International Confederation of Free Trade Unions (ICFTU). On the other hand, the Communist World Federation of Trade Unions (WFTU) welcomed the new movement in the Arab world, if only as a rival to the ICFTU: in contrast to the ICFTU, the WFTU had had only limited success in the area. The struggle of these three organizations for Arab labor's affiliation, of course, points to the growing importance of Arab labor in international affairs.

Important changes have taken place in the Arab world since my trip through the area in 1958 and since preparing the manuscript. Of paramount importance, it appears that the tide of direct Communistic influence is now ebbing throughout the Arab world and a general realignment is taking place. The pan-Arab labor movement, however, although disillusioned with the World Federation of Trade Unions, has not moved into the Western camp. On the contrary, if anything the pan-Arab movement has become more pro-Arab. Further, as a corollary to the general reorientation, the pan-Arab labor movement is replacing its former interest in developing an Afro-Asian federation with an interest in the neutralist pan-African movement. In the meantime, the international anti-Communist labor movements, which historically have been associated with the West, are also having some second thoughts about these critical areas. They are now in the process of broadening their bases so that, while they retain their anti-Communist character, they are becoming more truly international and less Western in representation. It is hoped that this study will serve as a helpful introduction for further research in these interesting fields.

Source materials in English, French, and Arabic have been used as far as possible to document the study. The lack of government statistics, however, or their inaccuracy where they existed, were unending causes of frustration. Interviews and correspondence, therefore, with Arab labor leaders and other qualified individuals in the Arab world were necessary. It would be difficult to list by name each of the persons contacted, but they are all remembered for their friendly cooperation and helpfulness. Nevertheless, the executives of the International Confederation of Arab Trade Unions (ICATU) in Cairo and Dr. Abou Alam, the United Arab Republic's Labor and Social Attaché in its Embassy in Washington, D.C., deserve special mention. They repeatedly provided me with information and materials.

Among those in the international labor field who have been most helpful were the executives of the ICFTU in Brussels and the International Federation of Petroleum Workers (IFPW); the Labor Attachés in the U.S. Consulates in the Near East and North Africa; and Messrs. B. S. Yane and Arnold Steinbach of the U.S. Department of Labor, Washington, D.C. Dr. Steinbach and Professors John Dunlop of Harvard University, Charles Issawi of Columbia University, and Yusif Sayigh of the American University of Beirut read the manuscript and offered many helpful criticisms and suggestions.

The opportunity to conduct the on-the-spot survey was provided through a Grant-in-Aid from the Social Science Research Council. A Research Fellowship at Harvard University, Center for Middle Eastern Studies, then allowed me the time, facilities, and academic counsel I required to complete the project. There Professor A. J. Meyer, Associate Director of the Center, took particular interest in the project. But I also enjoyed the friendly guidance and counsel of Professors H. A. R. Gibb, Director of the Center, D. W. Lockard, Associate Director, and George E. Kirk.

None of these I have mentioned, however, is responsible in any way for the statements, opinions, or conclusions, of this study. I have sought to present both an accurate and sympathetic picture. Where I have failed I am alone to be blamed.

Finally, I take this opportunity to acknowledge the work of Mrs. Kenneth Pease and Mrs. Dorothy Serieka who typed the manuscript.

Van Nuys, California W.A.B.
March, 1960

CONTENTS

LIST OF TABLES

PAN-ARABISM AND LABOR

I

THE SETTING FOR A PAN-ARAB LABOR MOVEMENT

On 24 March 1956 the first International Confederation of Arab Trade Unions was formed in Damascus, aiming at a membership of twenty million Arab workers from the borders of Iran to the Atlantic Coast.[1] Although this was the first formal attempt to unify the Arab labor movements, the idea at least had been articulated as early as 1947 at Haifa in the congress of the Arab trade unions in Palestine.[2] The Palestinian War put an end to the Palestinian Arab labor movement, but the strong feeling for an international Arab labor federation never died. Therefore, when a labor movement was organized in Jordan, its former Palestinian leaders re-issued the call to unite the Arab labor movements.

THE FRAME OF REFERENCE

For several reasons one was tempted to write off the new International Confederation of Arab Trade Unions (ICATU) at its birth. In the first place, a number of the Arab governments were openly antagonistic toward trade unions in general and had made no legislative provisions for them. Where the provisions did exist, the governments in many cases still exercised restrictive measures over the labor movements. Therefore, at the time of the Arabs' first international labor congress, trade unionism either did not exist at all or was severely curtailed in Algeria, Bahrain, Iraq, Kuwait, Saudi Arabia, and Yemen — countries specifically included in the International Confederation of Arab Trade Unions' plans for expansion.[3]

Second, most of the Arab countries are still largely underdeveloped economically, without the highly industrialized society normally associated in the West with trade unionism. Throughout the Arab world, between 70 and 80 per cent of the total population are still engaged in agriculture or in purely nomadic pastoral pursuits.[4] While "industrialization" generally connotes factory organization and urban employment, the concept must be broad enough to encompass some forms of large-scale agricultural production.[5] But land is usually worked in the Near East on a share-cropping basis,[6] which forms a most difficult basis for labor organization.[7] In addition, although the trend is currently the other way, trade union legislation existing in several Arab countries specifically denied agricultural wage earners the right to organize.[8]

In this environment, therefore, one would hardly expect to find well-developed collective labor action. As a matter of fact, on purely labor issues there was at this time a general lack in the entire Arab world of collective labor action. Moreover, this failure existed on the local, national, and international levels. Collective bargaining, for example, and concomitant collective agreements rarely existed. What often passed as a collective agreement was a statement signed by two parties to settle a couple of issues on an *ad hoc* basis. In effect, these were not collective agreements at all, but were more in the nature of the settlement of grievances.[9]

On the part of labor itself, the lack of trained labor leaders has been a deterrent to the development of trade unions and collective labor action. A number of Arab workers have been exposed from time to time to the international labor conferences of the International Labour Organization (ILO) in Geneva, to the ILO seminars in Istanbul, and to its technical aid programs in the Arab world. In addition, the World Federation of Trade Unions (WFTU) and the International Confederation of Free Trade Unions (ICFTU) have trained a few Arab labor leaders. For example, the latter has sponsored short leadership courses for its North African affiliates.

Nevertheless, adequate trade union leadership training programs exist today only in Egypt, Morocco, and Tunisia. By way of contrast, general ignorance of trade unionism itself is so profound in several other Arab states, even among the Arab petroleum workers, that the Arabic words "trade union" are quite often meaningless. This combined with chronic unemployment and underemployment tends to destroy worker solidarity which, of course, precludes prolonged strikes for labor gains.

Furthermore, collective action has also frequently been thwarted by control from above. One form this has taken has been company control of labor organizations, either by outright repression or by substituting other forms of company-controlled workers' organizations for trade unions. Votes for pro-management candidates for union offices are frequently "bought," when management's agents agree to pay the workers' back union dues. Trade union leaders themselves, however, frequently seek to use their union position as a stepping-stone to a good position in the company. Indeed, this is expected of them by their co-workers. In collective negotiations, the same person has been known to represent both management and the workers.[10]

Paternalistic Governments

The most common form of external control over organized labor movements in the Arab world, however, has been exercised by the governments. On the one hand, while they might tolerate trade unions to exist, the governments sometimes subject them to such close supervision and control, with the constant threat of either jailing the union leaders or suspending the unions' activities, as to render them ineffective bargaining agents for labor. This has been particularly true until recently of the Iraqi and Egyptian governments which were dominated by highly centralized political systems in control of reactionary landowners, who were inherently suspicious of labor unions as a revolutionary force.

On the other hand, governmental control has taken a new form in recent years in the Arab Near East. There is an increasing trend among the Arab governments themselves to establish and nurture labor movements. In the so-called McNair Report, Justice A. R. Cornelius notes the following:

> I have borne in mind that the extent of freedom from domination and control must be measured by very different standards in different conditions. Thus in one comparatively small region, viz. the Middle East, countries are found whose governments are at present engaged in bringing organisations of workers and employers into existence, both by education in trade union practice as well as by legislation. A degree of governmental influence is to be inferred which these organisations are probably powerless to resist. Yet it has to be conceded that it is an influence of a parental character, and the presumption of benevolence must be made in its favour.[11]

The most obvious danger in this arrangement, of course, and one which he points out, is that of domination or control by the government over the labor organization.[12] But while labor might expect this and fight back, it is impotent against a paternalistic government promulgating elaborate labor legislation by which the government really intends to benefit labor but instead, unintentionally, stifles collective labor action. In most instances, the elaborate labor codes usurp the position of collective agreements. Defending their action, the governments invariably argue that their labor legislation expresses mere minima which labor can and should improve upon in collective negotiations. In practice, however, this has unfortunately not been the case. Except in the very large establishments, inspection and enforcement agencies fail to enforce the minima. Therefore, in the small workshops the working day may be as long as twelve hours, in unsafe and unsanitary surroundings.[13]

Confronted with this anomaly, the government then frequently argues that in a sense the labor law's minimum standards are "targets" which the government hopes will obtain throughout the entire economy in the future. But in either case, whether the labor codes represent minima or targets, when large employers are faced with labor demands exceeding the law, they normally point to the double standard and often successfully invoke the labor law on the ground that they fulfill the *legal* requirements while others do not.

Until the labor laws are generally enforced, therefore, attempts at collective bargaining for a given trade or industry on a nationwide basis will be ineffectual. With good reason, one of the demands of several recent Near Eastern strikes has been that the labor laws be enforced.

THE FORM OF LABOR PROTEST

Trade unionism is a form of labor protest and is directly related to the process of industrialization. To be sure the Arab world is still comparatively unindustrialized. Yet it has made significant economic and industrial strides since World War II, largely through the prodigious increase in the production of petroleum.

While the petroleum industry is of paramount economic importance in the Near East, the labor-absorbing capacity of the industry itself is by its very nature limited. Therefore, except in small countries like Bahrain, Kuwait, and Qatar, the total number engaged in the petroleum industry represents only a small fraction of the total labor force.[14]

Nevertheless, the petroleum industry is the largest single employer of industrial workers in the Near East and is probably the most ideally suited, from the Western point of view, for labor organization. Except for Iraq, however, none of the Arab oil-producing states in the Persian Gulf has a petroleum workers' trade union. But here labor protest manifests itself in a variety of other forms. In the partially industrialized Persian Gulf area, although attempts have been made to establish trade unions, labor protest generally assumes the simpler and more direct forms of protest, such as absenteeism, malingering, sleeping on the job, sporadic work stoppages, and occasional general strikes.[15]

In the meantime, the traditional authority patterns found in family, tribe, and government have been transferred to industrial relations. This is a common phenomenon in the Near East where most "industrial workers" are really artisans, the hand workers in small craft shops. For that matter, one need only glance through recent Near Eastern industrial censuses [16] to see that the distinction between "entrepreneur" and "employee" hardly exists in these shops or is obscured by family ties.[17] In this close-knit, occupationally unstratified society, the agricultural worker looks to his landlord, the artisan to the master craftsman, and both to the local government official to resolve their personal and labor problems. Therefore, when the unsophisticated worker goes into a larger and more complex industry, he tends initially to transfer this traditional relationship to his foreman and, in cases of appeal, to the local government labor officer.[18]

The New Industrial Society

There is strong evidence, however, that the native crafts of the Near East are in the process of decline in the face of competition from cheaper mass-produced foreign imports and from products of large-scale mechanized industry at home. Fisher points out that this phenomenon which began in the textile industry is spreading to almost all trades.[19] At the same time, he indicates, labor conditions are getting worse, as in the first stages of the Industrial Revolution in Europe and America. Craft or "home" industry is degenerating into sweated labor, and labor legislation is often a dead letter because of lack of government inspection or control.

It must also be remembered that the newly committed industrial workers in the larger industries soon become veterans. For example, labor turnover has been reduced to a minimum in most of the oil companies. Even in the newer petroleum companies established since the end of World War II, the average Arab employee has several years' continuous service. But this does not mean that the worker is happy. His initial shift from a nomadic or agricultural to an industrial environment had been painful. He objected to rules and regulations being made without his participation which affected his duties, movements, and place of work. In fact, he probably walked off the job once or twice and went back to his old way of life before resigning himself to his niche in the new industrial society. He then begins to recognize a need for some new machinery to replace traditional relationships to settle problems of labor relations in his new industrial environment.

Therefore, despite its overwhelmingly disproportionate agricultural population, the Near East is developing a small but important industrial cadre. Even in the more isolated areas, the oil companies have employed thousands of Arab workers and trained them in technical skills and operations. For example, the Arabian American Oil Company alone, whose normal manpower numbers less than 15,000 Saudi Arab employees, estimates that it has employed in the course of its operations over 100,000 Saudi Arabs. This pattern, of course, has been repeated elsewhere in the Persian Gulf area. Many of these newly indoctrinated industrial workers have been absorbed in other industries which have developed in the wake of the flood of oil.[20]

Meanwhile the industrial workers throughout the Near East are becoming more sophisticated. With the exception of only a few, all the Arab countries have joined the International Labour Organization and have availed themselves of its technical services.[21] Various and sundry international trade union associations have wooed the Arab workers with offers of technical aid, literature, and invitations abroad. It has been estimated, for example, that in some of the Arab countries trade union leaders down to the fourth level have made at least one trip behind the Iron Curtain as guests of Communist trade unions. Most of the Arab labor leaders like to travel, however, and may have also made trips as guests of similar groups in the West.

Catalytic Agents

Perhaps the most important influence in developing labor consciousness in the backward areas has come through the impact on their societies of large groups of Egyptian, Lebanese, and Palestinian technical and professional workers, teachers, and government administrators, who have been recruited for work in the Persian Gulf states, Iraq, Libya, and Yemen. Their primary role has not been that of revolutionary agents, as has often been suggested, but rather of catalytic agents.

The Persian Gulf Arab, for example, initially found it difficult to identify himself with his fellow Western workers. Although he envied their higher standard of living, he never seriously imagined he could demand the same. However, when fellow Arabs from the Levant were brought in, whose standard of living was also higher than his own, he immediately identified himself with them and never hesitated a moment to demand similar treatment for himself. Therefore, the local Saudi Arab petroleum workers demanded and got both the salary differentials and the Special Leaves With Pay, which had been granted as "expatriate" bonuses to attract the Levantine Arabs from their native lands to work in Saudi Arabia's desert climate.

In addition, there are the Pakistani-Indian groups of workers. Both these and the imported Levantine Arabs have been public exponents of the advantages of labor organization in the backward areas, even though they may never have been trade union members back at home. However, being strangers in a foreign land, with none of the strong traditional family or kin relationships to rely upon, and having no real job security, they invoke the idea of some form of labor organization to defend their rights. In some of these states where trade unions are implicitly or explicitly forbidden, they have been able to organize themselves in the guise of clubs which, in effect, have been a form of labor organization.

THE CHARACTER OF PROTEST

Contrary to Western experience, labor movements do not require highly industrialized and occupationally stratified societies to thrive. In this connection, Lichtblau points out that in South Asia labor movements are thriving in predominately agricultural societies and in some areas have exceeded in size not only existing political parties, but also other social movements.[22] A similar phenomenon has occurred in the Arab world. One need only cite the more widely known Arab labor movements such as Morocco's

Union Marocaine du Travail (UMT), the largest in Africa, and Tunisia's *Union Générale des Travailleurs Tunisiens* (UGTT), not to mention the smaller movements which mushroomed overnight in backward Bahrain and nomadic Jordan.

Trade Unions and Nationalism

Trade union activities are ideally suited to the purposes of nationalists in colonial countries, for the Western colonial administrators accept trade unions as part and parcel of normal economic life. Moreover, socialist and trade union pressures at home can generally restrain colonial administrations from suppressing the labor movements, even when they engage in obvious political strikes and demonstrations.[23] In fact, numerous instances can be cited in which the colonial government's labor officers deliberately aided and abetted the local labor movement, in the expectation that with proper guidance under their aegis it would follow the development of Western labor movements.[24]

The suitability of the trade union movement to nationalistic ends has never been more apparent than in the North African struggles for independence, which still continue in Algeria. For example, both the International Confederation of Free Trade Unions (ICFTU) and the World Federation of Trade Unions (WFTU) openly supported the Moroccan and Tunisian nationalist labor movements in their struggles for national independence from France. This occurred in spite of the fact that most of the French metropolitan unions are members of one or the other international organization.[25]

In this same connection, it was also of interest that at the International Labour Conference in Geneva in June 1958, France's representative was careful to defend the French suppression of the Algerian trade union movement specifically on the basis of subversion and rebellion, not because it was a trade union movement. Nevertheless, the labor world as represented in public denunciations from leaders of the ICFTU, WFTU, AFL-CIO, ICATU, and other international organizations, feels rightly or wrongly that France is suppressing a legitimate labor movement, not a rebellion.[26]

For similar reasons, labor movements form ideal vehicles for social and political reformers. For example, during the period 1953–56 would-be reformers captured nascent labor movements in Saudi Arabia and Bahrain and led them in strikes which *The*

Economist said were directed primarily at the reactionary ways of the ruling family.[27] When the Saudi Arabian government issued its repressive anti-strike decree in 1956,[28] it aroused a storm of protests and world-wide sympathy for the movement. The ICFTU, among others, denounced the decree as "the worst type of feudal reaction" and forwarded a protest to the Secretary General of the United Nations (Saudi Arabia is not a member of the ILO), asking him to have it submitted to the Economic and Social Council for action.[29] International sympathy was also aroused and protests raised against repressive measures taken in Iraq, Jordan, and the Sudan against the labor movements.

"Normal" Trade Unionism

Various accusations have been made that the ICATU is primarily a political rather than a "normal" labor movement, and that it is using trade unionism as a facade to hide its real purposes. But ICATU has made no effort at all to hide its political orientation. The preamble to its Constitution states that "workers in the Arab fatherland believe in the unity of the Arab nation . . . the liberation of the Arab Nation from imperialist exploitation, and economic, political and social retrogression . . . ." [30] Shortly after his election as ICATU's first secretary general, Fathi Kamil reiterated that the new international labor confederation was intended to be the "true foundation of Arab solidarity." [31] A more recent semi-official statement paraphrases the movement's official position, as follows:

> I register for history before history forgets, that the establishing of ICATU was one of the fruits of the Arab struggle against imperialism, exploitation, and all domination whether internal or external.[32]

The new international is patently, almost defiantly, a nationalistic and reform movement. On the one hand, it is nationalistic in the sense that it is striving for complete political and economic independence. The ICATU feels that Britain and France have not fully reconciled themselves to the fact that the sovereignty of the Arab states is real and final. Recent or current examples which the ICATU cites are the conflicts over the Suez Canal, Algeria, Buraimi, Oman, and Yemen. On the economic front, the ICATU wants Arab industries to be run without foreigners and unbeholden to any foreign country.[33]

On the other hand, the movement also claims to be nationalistic in the Arabic sense of the word. The Arabs have two words for nationalism, one referring to the sentiment which flourishes within the frontiers of a country,[34] and the other signifying Arab "peoplehood."[35] The latter, which is often used in association with Arab nationalism, transcends the political slugging matches between Arab states and the rifts of public opinion. If a foreign statesman tries to pit the Arabs against each other, he pits *wataniyyah* against *qawmiyyah* and the latter is likely to win.[36] In this latter sense, the international Arab labor movement has stated that it is striving for Arab unification. As al-Mahdi states, the Arab workers have preceded their governments in uniting.[37]

EVALUATION

The International Confederation of Arab Trade Unions has not developed along Western lines. In fact, it cannot, for the "challenge" represented in the traditional explanations of the origin of Western trade movements does not exist on a large enough scale in the Near East to elicit a response of the magnitude represented in the Arab labor movements.[38] In its political bias, the ICATU is unlike Western labor organizations, for they are normally conceived of as pressure groups, as distinguished from political parties.

Is the International Confederation of Arab Trade Unions, therefore, abnormal and illegitimate? In a research project partly financed by the Ford Foundation, several eminent American labor economists conclude that in analyzing the labor problem a wider approach must be adopted which takes into account the varied experience of different countries.[39] The fact that trade union movements are different from Western patterns does not by itself make these movements abnormal or illegitimate.

On this basis, therefore, we will examine both the challenges which brought the ICATU into existence and the character of the pan-Arab labor movement itself as it has begun to develop.

II

THE INTERNATIONAL CONFEDERATION OF ARAB TRADE UNIONS

Trade unionism in the Arab world is a comparatively recent development. Labor organizations are not an entirely new phenomenon, however, for their beginnings can be traced in a few Arab countries to the turn of the century.[1] Nevertheless, the significant advances which these movements have made were generally achieved from the time of World War II to the present. In the meantime, however, some of these have mushroomed into large well-organized and efficient organizations, while others are still in their formative stages.

TABLE 1. ARAB LABOR ORGANIZATIONS

COUNTRY	UNION MEMBERSHIP
Aden	11,511
Algeria	320,000
Bahrain	. .
Egypt	275,000
Iraq	821
Jordan	11,248
Kuwait	. .
Lebanon	21,478
Libya	5,000
Morocco	880,000
Oman	. .
Qatar	. .
Saudi Arabia	. .
Syria	32,213
Sudan	54,335
Tunisia	226,000
Yemen	. .

Source: U.S. Department of Labor, Office of International Labor Affairs, *Directory of Labor Organizations, Africa*, and *Directory of Labor Organizations, Asia and Australasia* (Washington, 1958). Membership as of the end of the year 1957.

Both the ICFTU and WFTU have attempted to bring the Arab labor movements into their organizations and, of the two, the ICFTU has had considerably more success. In general, both have directed their efforts at the labor movements in the individual Arab states, although the ICFTU has also had a regional plan in mind. But the first attempt at uniting the Arab movements purely on the basis of Arab nationality is represented in the International Confederation of Arab Trade Unions.

In one sense, it does not represent an entirely new force in the Arab world, for organized labor has been a significant force in obtaining national goals in several Arab countries.[2] But in another sense, it is a radically new force because ICATU aims to make Arab labor an international force. In pursuing this mission, ICATU has had dealings in every Arab state, either in wooing the existing labor organizations to affiliate with it or in assisting labor in the backward areas to organize. Before tracing ICATU's impact upon labor throughout the Arab world, a very brief outline of its early history and development is required to understand it.

ORIGINS

The Federation of Labor Unions in Jordan initiated the proposal to form an independent Arab federation of trade unions. Following a series of discussions with labor leaders from Syria, and later from Egypt and Lebanon, Zaidan Yunus, the secretary general of the Jordanian federation, issued a statement on 2 December 1955 that agreement among labor leaders from these four countries had been reached to establish a federation.[3] Steps were then immediately taken to convene a congress of Arab trade unionists and to draft a constitution for the proposed federation. Shortly thereafter, the constituent committee approved a draft constitution and sent out invitations to labor leaders in Algeria, Egypt, Iraq, Jordan, Lebanon, Libya, Saudi Arabia, and the Sudan to attend the First Arab Labor Congress to be held on 22–24 March 1956 in Damascus.[4]

The Syrian government had indicated its support of the movement by allowing a credit of twenty thousand Syrian pounds for the congress. In addition, it provided all the necessary facilities for the conference. Moreover, a number of ministers and other responsible government officials attended the opening ceremonies, which were held in the auditorium of the Syrian University.[5] In a sense, it was fitting that the pan-Arab labor congress was convened in Damascus, for it was the birthplace of Arab nationalism.

It is interesting to note that observers from Iraqi and Tunisian labor organizations were reported present at the congress, and that telegrams in support of the movement were received from labor groups in Bahrain, Kuwait, and Saudi Arabia.[6] The telegrams probably came from individuals, for no legally recognized labor organizations existed at this time in these countries. Among the three, Bahrain came the nearest to having an organized movement; Kuwait had no organized group at all. Saudi Arabia had a self-appointed group at this time known as the "Committee Representing Saudi Workmen."

Delegations from only five Arab countries actually participated as founding members in the first congress, as follows: [7]

The All Egypt Trade Unions Congress.[8]
The Confederation of Trade Unions in Syria.
The Progressive Federation of Trade Unions in Damascus.
The Federation of Independent Trade Unions in the Lebanese Repubic.
The Federation of Trade Unions of Workers and Employees in North Lebanon.
The Federation of Trade Unions in Jordan.
The Libyan General Workers' Union.

ORGANIZATION

The International Confederation of Arab Trade Unions is organized along the general lines of other international labor organizations, as follows.

Congress and the Executive Council

According to the Constitution,[9] the ultimate authority of the International Confederation of Arab Trade Unions is to be vested in a representative congress, convening in ordinary session annually and in extraordinary session as required. To date, however, the congress has been convened only twice. The Second Arab Labor Congress was held in Cairo between 24–29 April 1959.[10] Earlier congresses had been postponed because of the unsettled conditions in the Arab world.

The congress is to consist of delegates from member organizations on a proportional basis according to their membership.

Nevertheless, no country can have less than four nor more than twelve delegates. Moreover, each country is allowed only one vote regardless of the number or size of the organizations. The pattern obviously is designed for monolithic labor organizations in each state. Apparently the intent was to encourage labor organizations in the individual Arab states to confederate.[11]

When the congress is not in session an executive council acts for and on its behalf.[12] It is supposed to meet in ordinary sessions twice a year and in extraordinary session at the request of the officers or the secretary general. Each member country has equal representation in the council, but the congress itself chooses the members in secret ballot. Their term of office is two years. The executive council elects from among its members all of the confederation's officers, with one notable exception, the secretary general. Congress elects him.

Officers

The executive council currently consists of twenty-two members, including the secretary general. The number will be increased, however, by five additional members: three from the Sudan Workers' Trade Union Federation (SWTUF) and two from the Federation of Trade Unions in Jordan. Their governments had refused to allow delegations to attend the recent congress in Cairo. From among these members the following officers were elected on 27 April 1959:[13]

President: Salim Shita, Libya.

He presides over meetings of the executive council and the congress, and is responsible for the proper conduct and discipline of meetings.

Vice-Presidents:
Sawi Ahmad Sawi, Egypt.
Muhammad Khalil al-Sharqawwi, Lebanon.
Yahya Judah al-Shibani, Iraq.

They deputize for the president in his absence, rotating according to alphabetical sequence of their names.

Secretary General: Muhammad As'ad Rajah, Egypt.

This is ICATU's most important single office. In a real sense its incumbent *is* the ICATU. He organizes and supervises directly the affairs of the general secretariat, and on a day-to-day basis ICATU's affairs. He functions as its official spokesman; initiates and signs all its correspondence and releases; controls its financial and administrative machinery. On his own, he can convene a meeting of the executive council. He is responsible for its agenda as well as that for the congress. He proposes the membership of three of ICATU's six committees.

Assistant Secretaries General:

Khalid al-Hakim, Syria.

Madhat Kusa, Lebanon.

'Imad al-'Aziz, Iraq.

'Ali al-Nafish, Libya.

They assist the secretary general in his duties and responsibilities, and alternately deputize for him in his absence.

Administrative Controller: Mansur 'Abd al-Mun'im, Egypt.

The Constitution leaves his functions undefined. Apparently he assists the president at meetings.

The officers who were elected in 1956 during the first congress had served for three years because of the failure to hold a second congress. It is of interest to note that an Egyptian has been re-elected to the all-powerful position of secretary general. It is also worth noting that the new president is a Libyan, whose national labor organization is also affiliated to the anti-Communist ICFTU. The former president had been from the Syrian region of the United Arab Republic.

Committees

The Constitution also provides for the formation of six committees which are subject ultimately to the congress, but in its absence to the executive council:[14]

1. *Finance Committee*: Supervises financial affairs; exercises financial controls; drafts the budget; prepares annual financial reports; proposes changes in financial arrangements. Membership: Elected by executive council.
2. *Organization Committee*: Exercises general administration and planning in field of trade union organization work within the ICATU itself and the unaffiliated or unorganized Arab countries. Membership: Elected by executive council.
3. *Social Committee*: Looks after social and cultural trade union activities. Membership: Elected by executive council.
4. *Propaganda Committee*: Undertakes all forms of publicity and propaganda. Membership: Proposed by secretary general, approved by executive council.
5. *International Relations Committee*: Establishes contacts with national and international labor organizations; represents ICATU officially in United Nations, Arab League, ILO, and other international and regional organizations. Membership: Proposed by secretary general, approved by executive council.

6. *Legislative Committee*: Studies Arab and international labor legislation and draws up legislative recommendations for submission to the Arab countries. Membership: Experts proposed by secretary general, approved by executive council.

ROLE OF THE ARAB LEAGUE [15]

The movement originally had two concurrent phases. One phase consisted of an unorganized popular attempt to create an Arab labor federation. Its leaders were trade unionists, spearheaded by labor leaders from Jordan who continued in this role up to the first congress over which, in fact, they apparently presided. The other phase consisted of an official attempt by the Arab League to unify labor legislation in the Arab countries.

The Arab League had been generally interested in the problem of Arab labor for some time prior to the establishment of ICATU. For example, ILO's Petroleum Committee which was established in 1945,[16] has covered various aspects of industrial, labor, and human relations in the petroleum industry since its first session in 1947.[17] Egypt and Iraq have been members of the committee and have passed its resolutions, recommendations, and other pertinent material to the Arab League's Department of Social Affairs. It in turn discusses them with representatives of the Arab states in its membership.[18]

In this regard, the Arab League's Department of Social Affairs apparently was primarily interested in following a program of cooperation with the under-developed countries in the Arab League, to help them develop minimum labor legislation. Therefore, in 1955 it reported that it had prepared a model labor law providing minimum standards for the Arab countries to follow in their own legislative programs.[19] The special committee assigned to this task indicated that they had made a comparative study of labor laws current in the Arab countries and had noted their shortcomings. In addition, they had taken into consideration the ILO conventions and recommendations in developing their own exemplar.[20]

EGYPT'S LIBERATION RALLY

Meanwhile, the new regime in Egypt had taken Egyptian labor under its protection. Trade unions had been supported previously by political leaders or parties, particularly the Wafd. But the attention which the Revolutionary Command Council gave labor was unprecedented in Egyptian history. While it attempted to control union activity, at the same time the new regime tried to win popularity among the working class. Therefore, within a very few months of its successful coup d'état in 1952, the new regime began promulgating legislation which was generally designed to encourage labor.

The net effect was to mobilize the Egyptian workers' support and allegiance to the goals of Egypt's official Liberation Rally, the mass organization created in support of the Revolutionary Command Council. Its special interest in Egyptian trade unions is reflected in the fact that it placed them under direct control of a labor section in the Liberation Rally headquarters. A retired army officer was placed at its head.

A LABOR BASE FOR PAN-ARABISM

During its first two years, 1952–53, the inexperienced Egyptian military junta had been preoccupied with domestic affairs. At the time, therefore, many Western observers felt that the new regime would continue to concentrate its efforts and attention on matters purely Egyptian. Moreover, on the same basis there were many who hopefully thought that Egypt would assume a pro-Western attitude, once the British forces had been evacuated from their bases on Egyptian soil in the Suez Canal Zone.

Once it had thoroughly consolidated its position at home, however, the new regime began to assume active leadership of the pan-Arab movement. Egypt's interest in the movement was especially fired, however, when it saw its leadership in the Arab world threatened by the Baghdad Pact.[21] Therefore, the idea of a pan-Arab labor federation, which was being pushed at the moment in an amateur fashion by the trade unionists, apparently appealed to Egypt as an ideal tool for developing mass support throughout the Arab world.

Well-organized popular fronts were not, of course, unknown in the Arab world. Nevertheless, one of the big differences between the North African and Levantine Arab struggles for national independence had been the fact that the North African popular fronts had had a broad base in organized labor. In fact, Morocco's Istiqlal Party had been largely ineffective until Tunisian labor leaders came in and helped organize a popular base for it among the workers. For that matter, both Tunisia's Neo-Destour

Party and Morocco's Istiqlal remained closely identified with their respective labor movements after achievement of their national independence.

Apparently Egypt intended to apply this principle on a broader scale and attempt to organize the entire Arab labor force in the interests of pan-Arabism. The junta's success in dealing with its own domestic labor movement, of course, was a proven fact. Moreover, the labor section of the Liberation Rally was ready and ideally equipped for the new task.[22] Therefore, when Egypt came along to sponsor the movement, the hitherto unorganized attempts to establish the federation were crowned with success. In the process, Egypt captured the new International Confederation of Arab Trade Unions at its first congress. Like the Arab League, the headquarters of the ICATU are located in Cairo.[23] The Egyptian government apparently helps finance its operations.[24]

INTERNATIONAL RESPECTABILITY

On 26 May 1958, the Arab League signed an agreement on cooperation between it and the International Labour Organization (ILO) which, among other things, will help the Arab League develop its labor legislation program.[25] It is true that the ILO has concluded similar agreements with other groups.[26] Nevertheless, its agreement with the Arab League had special significance. It provided the sought-after international recognition the Arab League wanted for the stepped-up regional labor program.[27]

In the meantime, while the Arab League was achieving international status on this basis, the International Confederation of Arab Trade Unions had also won international recognition by obtaining an invitation to attend the ILO's annual labor conference in Geneva. ICATU's delegates were not granted consultative status, which the ICFTU and the WFTU enjoy in the ILO. Nevertheless, they were granted observer status as representatives of a "Non-Governmental International Organization." [28]

Shortly after its establishment, the new Arab federation had added "International" to its name. Whether this was intended or not, recognition from the ILO has in a sense given the title proper endorsement in the Arab world. ILO recognition, for example, tends to enhance the pan-Arab ICATU's status among some of the Arab states.[29] Moreover, among certain classes of workers, it has been found that ILO recognition often connotes international, and even United Nations' sanction of the movement, its goals, and methods.

EGYPTIAN CONTROL

Naturally, accusations have been made that the Egyptians are using the pan-Arab labor movement for their own ends. G. L. Harris, for example, states in his recent book on Egypt that the ICATU is "significant as an instrument of the Nasser Government for exercising leadership in the Arab World."[30]

As much as some might oppose it, however, 'Abd al-Nasir apparently has met the qualifications of leadership in the field of pan-Arabism. To a considerable number of Arabs he has become the champion of Arabism (*batal al-'urubah*).[31] Therefore, what more natural development than the Egyptians assuming leadership of the pan-Arab labor movement? At any rate, ICATU's aims and philosophy should first be examined before final judgment is passed.

III

THE PHILOSOPHY OF THE INTERNATIONAL CONFEDERATION OF ARAB TRADE UNIONS

Article 6 of the Constitution of the ICATU gives a list of the new federation's aims.[1] The first of these sixteen aims is all-embracing: "Ensuring a better life for workers in the Arab fatherland and raising their standard of living." The next several also deal with problems directly related to labor; e.g., labor legislation, working conditions, labor productivity, industrial training and education, consumer cooperatives, unemployment, social security, and similar issues.

Thereafter, however, the aims are concerned with politics, nationalism, imperialism, self-determination, self-rule, independence, and world peace. Apparently, in the opinion of the International Confederation of Arab Trade Unions, these are of greater, or at least more immediate, concern to Arab labor than purely labor issues. In this regard, it should also be noted that the same pattern prevails in the resolutions issued from time to time by the executive council of the ICATU.[2]

At its second congress held in Cairo in March 1959, however, the ICATU passed a number of economic and social resolutions. Five of these dealt specifically with economic issues, and four with labor and social problems. Nevertheless, the remaining thirty-seven resolutions and recommendations were essentially concerned with political matters.

Why is the new movement oriented in this direction? An answer may be found in the following, which represents the most salient characteristics of the pan-Arab labor movement's philosophy.

UNITY OF THE ARAB WORLD

The preamble to the draft constitution underwent considerable revision before ICATU's first congress finally approved it.[3] In its final form,[4] however, it oriented the Arab labor movement unmistakably in the direction of Arab nationalism.

The fact that the congress was held in Damascus, the birthplace of Arab nationalism, undoubtedly provided the movement with its dominant theme, Arab unity. Charles Issawi has pointed out in this regard that Syria was the first country to proclaim in its Constitution that it was a part of the Arab nation, a step followed by Egypt six years later.[5] Quite naturally, therefore, the Damascus congress revised the draft constitution to incorporate this same theme.

In essence, therefore, the preamble to the Constitution presents two fundamental concepts which are designed to dominate the Arab workers' entire philosophy: (1) the concept of the unity of the Arab nation; and (2) the concept of a labor mission (*risalah*) to promote unification of the Arab nation.

Uniting Organized Labor

Within this framework, the paramount task of the newly-formed labor confederation was to unite Arab labor. The most obvious place to begin this task, of course, from the standpoint of ease, would be in those areas where labor movements were already organized. To be sure, the ICATU had drawn organized affiliates from five Arab countries in its first sweep.[6] Nevertheless, there were still the large and important North African labor organizations in Morocco and Tunisia to be won over.[7] In addition, there were the smaller but nevertheless organized labor movements in Aden, Iraq, Lebanon,[8] and the Sudan. All of these were specifically included in the ICATU's definition of the Arab world to be united.[9]

The ICATU had associated itself from the beginning with the Arab League as its unofficial regional labor arm.[10] It was suggested, in fact, that the Arab League endorse the movement. At that time, however, the movement probably would not have won the membership's approval. At any rate, pressure apparently was brought to bear upon the Arab governments to recognize the ICATU as the competent and representative regional labor organization for the Arab world. In the meantime, the ICATU has sought and won international status in the ILO as a regional labor organization.

The International Confederation of Arab Trade Unions embarked upon its appointed mission without delay. It carried on correspondence with the labor leaders in the unaffiliated Arab countries; it arranged exchange visits; it attended their trade union conferences; and in turn it invited them as observers to its own meetings. In the three years the ICATU has existed, a number of Arab labor organizations have cooperated on this fraternal basis. To date, however, only the Sudan Workers' Trade Union Federation (SWTUF) has formally affiliated with the new movement.

Groundwork in the Unorganized Areas

Relatively important industrial and commercial labor forces are being developed in Bahrain, Kuwait, Saudi Arabia, and Yemen, largely through the impact of the petroleum industry upon their economies. Nevertheless, labor still remains unorganized. There are a number of factors, to be sure, to account for this condition. But without any doubt, the largest single deterrent to organized labor has been the express, or tacit, government disapproval of trade unions. Government opposition to the pan-Arab labor movement naturally followed in due course.

It is obvious, therefore, that the ICATU has no affiliates in the Persian Gulf area. Nevertheless, the pan-Arab labor movement continues to press its mission in the unorganized states. For example, the ICATU passed the following resolutions relative to Saudi Arabia at its second congress held in Cairo in April 1959:

1. We demand freedom of association in Saudi Arabia for trade unions to protect the rights of the workers and to represent them in the International Confederation of Arab Trade Unions.
2. We demand the repatriation of the Arab workers who were deported and deprived of their nationality.
3. We demand that labor legislation be issued for the protection of the workers from oppression and injustice, and that present reactionary legislation be canceled.

In the meantime, however, the pan-Arab labor movement apparently recognized that organization drives are futile without the proper legal framework to build upon. The ICATU has, therefore, stressed the importance of labor legislation and has scored on this point in almost all of the unorganized states. At the time of the confederation's founding in 1956, for example, only Saudi Arabia had a labor code of sorts. In the other states of the Persian Gulf, industrial relations have been generally handled on an *ad hoc* basis.

Fortunately, serious efforts had already been made to develop good labor legislation for the Arab world. The International Labour Organization, for example, and the Arab League had both been interested in the subject and had sought to lay the groundwork for sound legislative efforts. In fact, their cooperative efforts in the area were formalized by an agreement in the spring of 1958.

They have cooperated, for example, in preparing a collection of Arabic terms dealing with social security, in order to unify terminology in the Arab states. In addition, the two agencies have combined efforts to translate the ILO's conventions into Arabic.[11] These then are urged upon the Arab governments as universally accepted patterns to be followed in their own legislation. Basic among the ILO conventions, of course, is freedom of association for labor — an essential of particular importance to the success of the ICATU's program in these unorganized states.

Promising Developments in Labor Legislation

The success of these efforts in the unorganized areas can be measured by the fact that new labor legislation has since been promulgated in Bahrain and Iraq.[12] Both governments might hesitate to credit the International Confederation of Arab Trade Unions with any significant role in the development of their labor laws. Nevertheless, strong evidence indicates the direct influence of the ICATU upon the development of the Bahrain labor code.[13] Moreover, the indirect influence of the Arab League's Department of Social Affairs can be seen in the final development of Iraq's recent labor legislation.[14]

At any rate, it should be noted that both are progressive pieces of labor legislation. For the first time in its history, Bahrain granted legal recognition to labor unions. Although Iraqi legislation had done this as far back as 1936,[15] its new legislation provides the labor movement with more advantages than it previously had. An interesting feature in this regard is the stipulation requiring the formation of trade unions in establishments employing more than a hundred employees.[16]

Promising groundwork to legalize trade unions has also been laid in Kuwait. A few years ago it enlisted the services of a labor expert, on loan from the Egyptian Ministry of Social Affairs and

Labor, to draft a labor law. The law has not yet been promulgated. Nevertheless, it exists in draft form and is now in the process of being molded into final form. Of particular interest is the fact that the draft form of the law, which appeared in a government publication in 1957, guarantees freedom of association to employees.[17]

Much still remains to be done along these lines, however, in Saudi Arabia, Yemen, and Qatar. Of the three, Saudi Arabia alone has a labor code, but with no provisions for trade unions. The government, however, cannot hold out much longer on this point against the demands of both its restive labor force and the younger progressive government officials. Yemen is probably the least industrialized of all the independent Arab states and, therefore, has the least justification to promulgate labor legislation. Oil-rich Qatar, however, apparently needs labor legislation for its growing labor force. Its government has been considering drafting labor regulations.

Trade Union Consciousness

On the one hand, there is government opposition to labor organization in these unorganized states. On the other hand, however, there is the ignorance of labor itself regarding trade unionism. One of the ICATU's stated aims, therefore, is to make Arab labor trade union conscious. A number of means have been used.

The Arab federation has the usual organs of propaganda, such as trade union periodicals, tracts, and pamphlets. In the printed field, however, the ICATU's ablest propaganda vehicle has been the Egyptian newspapers, which are avidly read throughout the Persian Gulf states. A number of these regularly carry a column devoted to labor and trade union news, but all of them carry general news on labor developments. In addition, the United Arab Republic's powerful radios cover the labor scene.

Personal contacts between the ICATU and local labor have been generally conducted on a one-way basis. The mere fact that they are trade union leaders, of course, makes the ICATU's representatives *persona non grata* in the unorganized states. Nevertheless, a number of potential labor leaders from these areas make their way to Cairo. In fact, some of them have become permanent guests of the ICATU, after being banned from their own countries for illegal activities.

In the meantime, however, some of the ablest missionaries of trade unionism in these areas have been the social and labor experts who have been brought in to assist the governments. Both Saudi Arabia and Kuwait, for example, have a number of Egyptian experts assisting in the establishment of labor and social affairs activities. In this regard, it has been interesting to note the number of articles on industrial relations which have appeared in Kuwait publications. The last of a well-written series of five articles, for example, outlined the importance of trade unions in industry.[18] It is of interest, of course, that the article was written by an Egyptian. But the article is especially noteworthy, because it was carried in a publication of the government, which does not allow trade unions to exist in Kuwait.

LIBERATING THE ARAB NATION

According to the International Confederation of Arab Trade Unions, colonialism is the greatest obstacle to Arab unity. The pan-Arab labor movement has been, therefore, concerned with alleged Western "imperialism" and the means it uses to perpetuate its hold upon the area; viz., the Baghdad Pact; Point IV aid; military bases; and economic "exploitation" of Arab oil. In particular, the Eisenhower Doctrine has annoyed pan-Arabists.[19] They consider it an insult, that it implies a vacuum which Arab nationalism itself is unable to fill. More basically, however, they feel that the Eisenhower Doctrine poses a new obstacle to Arab unification by guaranteeing the status quo.

Within the past year, however, the pan-Arab labor movement has come to recognize that imperialism is not a Western monopoly. Whereas Western imperialism dominated the first congress of the International Confederation of Arab Trade Unions in 1956, it would be safe to say that the threat of international Communism was paramount in the second congress held in Cairo in April 1959.

Anti-Imperialism

The second congress, therefore, reaffirmed the policy of positive neutrality and non-alignment with either the Western or Eastern camps. Relative to these two, the ICATU now sees them as two phases of the same problem. On the one hand, the ICATU aims at the eradication from the Arab world of the vestiges of Western colonialism. On the other hand, the ICATU wants to prevent a new master from taking the place of the former colonial masters.

As a general principle, the ICATU states its recognition of a people's right to self-determination and its intention to support national independence movements.[20] A different principle, however, apparently underlies the ICATU's active support of the Arab movements. In essence, the principle involved is that the Arab states are parts of one indivisible Arab nation.

President 'Abd al-Nasir clearly articulated this principle, for example, in justification of the UAR's interference in Iraq's internal affairs; viz., the Communist infiltration of Iraq constituted a violation of Arab unity and of the Arabhood of Iraq. In this regard, President 'Abd al-Nasir has stated:

> We are one Arab Nation. Both our Constitution and the Iraqi Provisional Constitution provide in their articles that we are one Arab Nation. Accordingly, every Arab state has the right to defend Iraq's Arabhood and independence from Britain, the USA, the USSR, and all other countries. We are one Arab family in a boat caught in a tempest of international politics. If one member tears a hole in the bottom, are we expected to remain indifferent? [21]

Following this principle, the ICATU has also actively supported the Algerian struggle for independence from France,[22] and various nationalistic movements against the British Empire in the Persian Gulf and Trucial states. Similarly, the ICATU was involved in the affairs of Jordan and Lebanon during the civil disturbances in 1958.[23]

A New Force in the Struggle

The Arab confederation first made its mark in the world in connection with the nationalization of the Suez Canal. On 10 August 1956, during the height of the crisis over nationalization, the executive council of the ICATU convened an emergency meeting in Cairo.[24] It reached two main decisions regarding the crisis. One of these called for a general strike in the Arab world on August 16 to protest against the London Conference which had been called to resolve the Suez dispute, but without Arabs in attendance.

Generally speaking, the strike was not the success reported in the Arab press. Nevertheless, there was a scattered response throughout the Arab world. In the course of its protests, however, the ICATU was able to enlist considerable support in the non-Arab world. In particular, the Eastern bloc and the Communist-dominated World Federation of Trade Unions supported Egypt's stand on the Suez Canal.[25]

The executive council's second decision resolved that if Egypt were attacked, the Arab workers would immediately embark upon a campaign of sabotage against the West. Therefore, when Britain, France, and Israel invaded Egypt several weeks later, the Arab workers moved to carry out this decision. Apparently the oil pipeline in Syria had been designated as a primary target for sabotage. However, others beat the workers to it and destroyed the pump stations, effectively halting the flow of crude oil from Iraq to the Mediterranean — and Europe, for several months.

The magnitude of this deed practically obscured the smaller acts of sabotage committed in the oil installations in Kuwait and Qatar. Plans had also been made to render ineffective the Western military bases in Jordan and Libya, and to cut Western air and sea communications in the Arab world. To be sure, only a modicum of success was achieved. Nevertheless, in the Sudan the response of the SWTUF was great enough to force the government to declare a state of emergency.[26] Indirectly, Saudi labor also forced the Saudi Arabian government to shut off the flow of Saudi crude oil to the Bapco refinery on Bahrain Island, to prevent it from falling into the hands of the British during this period of strained relations.

On numerous occasions the ICATU has publicly and proudly claimed sole responsibility for these acts.[27] Its claims are exaggerated both as to the extent of sabotage effected and the degree of its own responsibility in perpetrating the sabotage. Nevertheless, the fact emerges that the voice of united Arab labor cannot henceforth be regarded as an empty threat, particularly with respect to Arab petroleum. At any rate, the token demonstration of what united labor can do has been a factor in spreading the idea of the importance of achieving Arab labor solidarity. In the meantime, of course, this new force has been exploited several times for political ends.[28]

SECURING SOCIAL JUSTICE

Labor itself presents a dichotomy in the philosophy of the International Confederation of Arab Trade Unions, for labor is both a problem and a means to an end. To be sure, conditions vary from country to country. Nevertheless, the general lot of the Arab worker is very poor compared with Western standards. In all of the Arab countries, for example, at least one or more of the following exist: large-scale unemployment or underemployment; low wages; oppressive conditions of work; complete absence of social security provisions; and inadequate or complete lack of labor legislation. From this point of view labor itself is a big problem.

The wage rates given in Table 2 represent perhaps one of the lowest wage scales in the Arab world. Nevertheless, the rate for common labor is not much lower than that prevailing in several other Arab states.

TABLE 2. WAGE RATES IN THE EASTERN ADEN PROTECTORATE

OCCUPATION	WAGE RATES	
	Shillings	Dollars
Laborer	5–8 a day	$0.71–1.13
Carpenter	15–16 a day	2.12–2.26
Mason	13–15 a day	1.83–2.16
Driver	150–350 a month	21.17–49.40
Soldier	150 and rations a month	21.17
Clerk (Government)	150–300 a month	21.17–42.34
Clerk (Civilian)	200–400 a month	28.23–56.46
Teacher	220–510 a month	31.05–71.98
Head of Government Department	450–800 a month	63.51–112.91

Source: U.S. Department of Labor, Bureau of Labor Statistics, *Labor Developments Abroad* (April 1959), p. 20. In addition, there is no labor department, labor legislation, or social security provisions. In contrast, of course, labor in some of the other Arab countries, particularly in the petroleum industry, enjoys a wage scale which compares very favorably with those prevailing in parts of Europe.

The Arab confederation has the usual aims of ordinary trade union organizations to combat labor ills.[29] Nevertheless, the International Confederation of Arab Trade Unions is predominantly a political movement. To all intent and purposes, the ICATU has relegated "normal" trade union aims to a secondary place in its program, subordinating them to its self-appointed primary mission of "liberating" the Arab nation. At first glance, therefore, the movement seems to have missed the real purpose of being a "labor" movement.

The preamble to its Constitution, however, states that the achievement of the workers' rights "depends upon the liberation of the Arab Nation from imperialist exploitation, and from economic, political, and social backwardness." Liberation, therefore, has also the connotation of social reform. The movement's efforts are to be directed against reactionary and feudalistic shackles, as well as against imperialism.

The Constitution specifically mentions in this regard the suppression of the freedoms of opinion and expression, the denial of democratic liberties, and various forms of discrimination. Moreover, the second congress of the ICATU did not hesitate to condemn publicly and pointedly the Arab "princes and their relatives" who squander fortunes on "pleasure and delights." In addition, the second congress decided to establish a permanent committee, attached to the directorate general of the ICATU in Cairo, to study labor conditions in the Arab world.[30]

In summary, the pan-Arab labor movement labors under the conviction that "normal" trade unionism in the backward areas would be a waste of time until social reforms have been introduced. As a matter of fact, trade unionism itself is impossible in these areas until social reforms are introduced to permit unions to exist.

PROMOTING INDUSTRIAL DEVELOPMENT

According to the pan-Arab labor movement's philosophy, liberation from foreign economic "exploitation" is impossible without compensatory large-scale Arab industrialization. Therefore, the ICATU has endorsed a number of programs to accelerate the pace of industrialization in the Arab nation. The second congress of the ICATU, for example, adopted specific resolutions in support of the following: economic planning for the Arab nation as a unit; the Arab Development Bank; tariff protection for Arab industry; and development of an Arab economic community.

COMPLEMENTARY ECONOMIES

The unity of the Arab nation is the fundamental tenet of the philosophy of the International Confederation of Arab Trade Unions. Accordingly, it endorses unified economic planning for the Arab world. Natural resources, for example, are to be pooled in "one unit in the service of the Arab group of nations. . . ." In addition, the ICATU endorses the proposed Arab common market, in emulation of the European common market. The labor movement also supports the Arab Development Bank, which is patterned after the International Bank for Reconstruction and Development. The Arab Bank is sponsored by the Arab League, and its capital stock is to be subscribed by member states of the Arab nation.

The absence in the ICATU's resolutions of any encouragement of foreign capitalization of industrial development is not an oversight. On the contrary, the ICATU endorses the use of Arab wealth to capitalize industrialization. Arab oil, of course, is paramount in these plans: "Arab oil is the most important natural wealth of the Arab Nation and should be used in the service of this Nation, for the improvement of its peoples' living standard and for the carrying out of its plans for economic development." (Resolution of the second congress.)

The Arab confederation has not endorsed nationalization of the oil industry. Moreover, it has not indicated how the oil wealth should be distributed, other than through subscriptions of stock in the Arab Development Bank. Nevertheless, the ICATU jealously guards Arab oil as an Arab resource and has taken a proprietary interest in it. The confederation considers the present concessionary agreements, for example, as prime examples of Western economic imperialism. Therefore, the ICATU has pledged itself to economic warfare with the "imperialist exploiters" in the oil-producing states.[31]

Technical and Management Skills

The Arab world has natural resources, a developing market, and potential capital in the form of oil wealth. But the fourth element, technical and management skills, is lacking for broad industrial development. The Arab world has been forced to rely upon foreigners for these skills, as it has been forced to rely upon them for capital in large-scale industrial projects. Indeed, by virtue of these factors alone, foreigners have perforce come into control of entire industries. The petroleum industry and the Suez Canal are the most obvious examples.

Some of these companies, however, have been accused of perpetuating their control by their unwillingness to hand over important operations to nationals.[32] In all fairness, such accusations have not been completely unjustified.[33] The International Confederation of Arab Trade Unions supports "Arabization" of such industries. To this end, it strongly endorses vocational, professional, and technical training programs for Arab workers.

STRENGTHENING WORLD PEACE

The pan-Arab labor movement has pledged itself to "support any effort exerted to spread and strengthen peace." Generally speaking, this means following the positive neutralism of President 'Abd al-Nasir.

Quite naturally, Zionism is considered the most imminent threat to world peace. The ICATU, therefore, has repeatedly called upon the workers of the world to unite with it in crushing Israel and restoring Palestine to the Arabs. The ICATU has had some success in this regard. For example, it has issued joint statements with other labor groups from the Eastern bloc in support of the Arab position in the dispute.

In addition, it has been recently decided to form a general federation for Palestinian workers. Apparently it is to be an independent body affiliated to the International Confederation of Arab Trade Unions and would be represented at all conferences and international meetings. The new federation would serve to bring the Palestine question to the notice of international labor.

IV

CONSOLIDATION OF THE PAN-ARAB LABOR MOVEMENT

The pan-Arab labor movement was launched in 1956 by trade union representatives from five Arab countries: Egypt, Jordan, Lebanon, Libya, and Syria. In 1957, the Sudan Workers' Trade Union Federation (SWTUF) was accepted as an affiliate. These countries, therefore, constitute the base of the pan-Arab labor movement. To the west lies the Arab Maghreb (Tunisia, Algeria, and Morocco) and to the east the oil-producing states of the Arab world. The pan-Arab labor movement has sought to expand in both directions and, in some respects, has made significant progress. In the meantime, however, without forgetting its broader mission, the pan-Arab labor movement has sought to consolidate its position at home.

The following is intended only as a survey of the pan-Arab aspects of the labor movement and is not designed to provide a detailed study of the labor movement in each country. The historical background and notes are only incidental to the main purpose of demonstrating the growing importance of the Arab labor movements' nationalistic and pan-Arab tendencies. Because of their different origin, development, and character, the labor movements of the Egyptian and Syrian regions of the United Arab Republic are treated separately.

THE EGYPTIAN REGION OF THE UAR

The Egyptian labor movement has the longest history and the largest membership of all the affiliates of the International Confederation of Arab Trade Unions. Even apart from this, however, Egyptian trade unionism has set the pattern which will probably be followed by a number of other Arab countries. The pattern is dissimilar from Western-style trade unions.

TRADE UNION DEVELOPMENT AND ORGANIZATION[1]

Although the Egyptian labor movement had its beginnings in the latter part of the nineteenth century, it had no significant development until much later. Abou Alam, for example designates World War I as the "training period" for Egyptian labor. It was not until 1942 during World War II, however, that the Egyptian government passed the first trade union law giving workers freedom of association.[2] In effect, this was the beginning of the Egyptian trade union movement as it exists today.

Shortly after the revolution in 1952, the new government promulgated Trade Union Act No. 319, which was designed to eliminate the harsher elements of the previous law.[3] For the first time, it allowed agricultural workers to organize. In addition, the act lowered the minimum membership from fifty to thirty to form a labor union, thereby broadening the base of the labor movement. The act also provides that when a union represents three-fifths of an establishment's labor force, the rest are automatically considered members and a compulsory check-off (for dues) is allowed. This provision in particular has contributed to union growth.

TABLE 3. NUMBER OF EGYPTIAN TRADE UNIONS AND THEIR MEMBERSHIP

YEAR	NUMBER OF TRADE UNIONS	MEMBERSHIP	AVERAGE MEMBERSHIP
1944	210	102,876	..
1945	189	89,560	..
1946	488	95,538	196
1947	441	91,604	208
1948	478	124,094	260
1949	465	123,005	264
1950	491	149,434	304
1951	448	..	..
1952	568	159,608	281
1953	947	265,192	280
1954	1154	..	..
1955	1155	394,245	341
1956	1249	459,029	370

Source: Egyptian Ministry of Social Affairs and Labor, Directorate General of Labor, *Census of Labor Unions and Federations in the Republic of Egypt, December 1956* (in Arabic; Cairo: Government Press, n.d.), p. 24.

The 1956 census of trade unions lists seventy unions with over a thousand members each, and eight with over five thousand members. Nevertheless, the Egyptian trade unions are small, averaging only 370 members in 1956. Most of Egypt's trade unions are "house" unions, in the sense that one union represents all of the workers within an establishment. (Quite often, however, there may be two "house" unions within the same establishment: one for manual *workers* and the other for white-collar *employees*.) The 1956 census reported a total of 904 *active* unions, of which only 292 were true craft unions. This feature has been considered a weakness, because the predominance of work unions over craft unions leads naturally to smaller unions.[4]

The small size of individual unions, however, has been compensated for by the creation of federations. The 1956 census listed forty-nine federations comprising 398 unions. The present regime, however, has been recently encouraging the creation of federations. Therefore, in November 1958, it was announced that the number had grown to 121 federations.[5] The textile workers', the petroleum and chemical workers', and the transportation workers' unions have three of the largest and most influential federations.[6]

With the assistance of the labor section of the Liberation Rally, an "All Egypt Trades Union Congress" was established in 1955. In effect, this took the place on an unofficial basis of a confederation; e.g., it represented Egyptian labor at international labor conferences in Damascus and Accra. In January 1957, however, the Trades Union Congress was reorganized into the Egyptian Confederation of Labor, comprising fifteen federations and two unions. By November 1958, its membership reportedly had grown to 121 labor federations and two unions.

The Government's Role

Under the present regime, the Labor Department handles all routine labor matters. The more important trade union problems and labor disputes, however, are handled in the labor section of the National Union Party, the regime's all-embracing political apparatus and the successor to the Liberation Rally. The labor section is headed by Major 'Abd Allah Tu'aimah, a retired army officer.[7] On the one hand, he controls the trade union leaders; only active members of the National Union may serve as officials of trade unions.[8] On the other hand, through his contacts with other army officers who now occupy posts in the government and industry, he can deal persuasively with industry. Therefore, the labor section has been an effective agency in keeping the labor peace.

The controls are intended to harness the nation's work force in a drive for rapid industrialization. Implicit in this arrangement, however, has been the end of free trade unionism, such as had existed. Reportedly, one of Egypt's leading protagonists of free trade unionism, Anwar Salamah, resigned in protest from the presidency of the Egyptian Confederation of Labor.[9] It must be remembered, however, that Egyptian trade unions have not developed from a free labor movement; they have developed under the protection of a paternalistic government. Therefore, although they have not been completely government controlled, present trade unions have been aptly characterized as government-nurtured "hot-house plants." [10]

Nevertheless, Egyptian labor has made significant strides forward under the new regime. Labor did not, however, win these concessions by joining forces with the government. On the contrary, it was the government which joined forces with labor to help it fight its fight against the hitherto more powerful employers. In return, therefore, the government expects a docile labor movement and labor peace.[11] At any rate, Egyptian labor has not had to exercise the conventional means of collective bargaining or strikes to obtain its goals.

In fact, Proclamation No. 75 of 1940 had outlawed strikes in public utilities and most manufacturing industries without permission of the Minister of Supply. The new regime, however, adopted a stricter attitude toward strikes and practically precluded the possibility of strikes occurring by means of its Conciliation and Arbitration Act of 1952. To put teeth in its attitude, the government then made strike leaders subject to court martial by a military tribunal (Military Court Order No. 54 of 7 December 1952).

In consequence, labor unrest has been resolved at times by rather stern methods in the interest of the State. At a very early stage in its rule, for example, the government demonstrated very pointedly its disapproval of strikes: the Communist leaders of a strike at Kafir al-Duwar were hanged in August 1952.[12]

While labor strikes still occur under the new regime, they occur with far less frequency than formerly. There were forty-nine strikes registered in 1950, for example, seventy-six in 1951 (the last full year under the old regime), thirty in 1952, three in 1953, and only two in 1954. To be sure other labor strikes have taken place, but they have not been publicized and their occurrence has been camouflaged in the press. On the other hand, political strikes take place on call and are widely publicized to demonstrate mass support of a given national policy.

In the meantime, however, the government also restricts lockouts. Moreover, at about the same time that the government outlawed strikes, it ordered industrialists not to discharge workers. But even without this additional safeguard, the workers' protection against arbitrary discharge and layoff had been materially improved by Law No. 317 of 1952: Individual Contracts of Employment.[13] At the same time the new regime had set up improved conciliation and arbitration machinery to settle labor disputes.

To be sure, the workers lost an important weapon in their struggle for labor gains when they lost the right to strike. Nevertheless, in some respects the new regime provided economic and social gains to labor which it would have found difficult to match by following conventional methods.[14]

Egyptian Labor and Pan-Arabism

The present regime recognizes the potential economic and political importance of labor. Indicative of the latter at the national level is the fact that in 1957 the government allowed thirty candidates of the Egyptian Confederation of Labor to stand for election to the National Assembly.[15] In fact, the government granted the president of the confederation the special favor of standing unopposed for election to the Assembly, a privilege which put him on a plane with cabinet members. The present regime's interest in the pan-Arab labor movement, therefore, is not an unnatural extension of its interest in Egyptian labor.

In the field of international labor, the Egyptian labor movement apparently is supposed to confine itself as far as possible to the International Confederation of Arab Trade Unions. To be sure, Egyptian labor may have fraternal relations and exchange visits — under government approval — with other international trade union organizations. Nevertheless, it cannot formally affiliate itself with them. Therefore, the international policies and program of the Egyptian labor movement are practically identical to those of the Egyptian-sponsored ICATU.[16]

But in the meantime, Egyptian labor leaders have dominated

the International Confederation of Arab Trade Unions. To a large extent they have determined its course. For this reason, the treatment of the Egyptian labor movement has been somewhat more extensive than that given the other national labor movements. Moreover, Egyptian labor has set a pattern which will undoubtedly be followed by many of these movements.

THE SYRIAN REGION OF THE UAR

The Syrian labor movement is of particular interest because it reflects the full implications of Egypt's pan-Arab labor program. Complete unity of the two regions of the United Arab Republic, however, has not yet been accomplished. For example, at the time of writing, the Syrian Labor Code of 1946 is in general still in effect. Moreover, the trade union organizations of the two regions are still independent and retain their old organizational patterns, although a proposed unification has been announced. Nevertheless, enough evidence is available to indicate the pattern Syrian labor will follow in the UAR.

Trade Union Development and Organization [17]

The origins of trade unionism in Syria can be traced as far back as World War I. Syrian trade unionism as it is known today, however, has developed only since World War II. Full legal recognition was not granted trade unions until 11 June 1946.[18] Immediately thereafter a number of trade unions registered with the government and by 1957 there were 281 registered trade unions.

Nevertheless, the Syrian labor movement did not develop into a powerful force. In the first place, much of the labor force still remains unorganized. The agricultural workers, for example, were not granted freedom of association under the Labor Code of 1946. Although they were guaranteed this right in the Syrian Constitution of 1953, agricultural labor was not included in the published lists of authorized occupations. Moreover, much of the non-agricultural labor force of 130,000 also remains unorganized.[19] In the second place, the labor movement itself is deceptively strong. A number of the unions are paper unions; although registered, they are inactive. In addition, the average trade union is small, averaging only 129 members in 1956.

The labor movement in the Syrian region of the UAR has

TABLE 4. NUMBER OF SYRIAN TRADE UNIONS AND THEIR MEMBERSHIP

YEAR	NUMBER OF TRADE UNIONS	MEMBERSHIP	AVERAGE MEMBERSHIP
1947	60	..	..
1948	105	..	..
1949	127	..	..
1950	149	..	..
1951	182	27,253	150
1952	190	27,391	144
1953	199	27,612	139
1954	219	30,261	138
1955	..	..	..
1956	256	32,943	129
1957	281	..	..

Sources: Figures for the earlier years through 1950 are from Republic of Syria, Ministry of National Economy, *Statistical Abstract of Syria, 1955* (Damascus: Government Press, 1956) and for the later years from Bureau des Documentations Syriennes et Arabes, *Étude sur la Syrie Économique*, 1957 (Damascus, n.d.).

several basic organizational differences from the labor movement in the Egyptian region. In Syria (and Lebanon), for example, mixed employer/employee associations exist, organized as trade unions. Stauffer points out, however, that they are in fact associations of small entrepreneurs with the problems of small entrepreneurs instead of trade unions.[20] Also unlike the Egyptian labor movement, labor in Syria is organized on a regional basis with a *general* labor federation in each district (*Muhafadhah*). At the end of 1957, there were eight general federations.[21] But in addition, there are both regional and national *industrial* federations, grouping together trade unions of one trade or industry. There were eighteen at the end of 1957. Finally, the Syrian Labor Code provides for a general labor confederation of all districts. The Confederation of Trade Unions in Syria was formed in 1948.

SYRIAN LABOR IN THE UAR

Shortly after the establishment of the United Arab Republic, a constituent committee of labor leaders from both regions of the UAR was formed to work out details of a merger of the Syrian and Egyptian labor movements. So far the merger has not been accomplished, apparently due to the incomplete unification of the two national economies and the desire to establish the trade union machinery of the National Union Party in Syria, as in Egypt. Nevertheless, the merger was to have been completed by the first of November 1959.[22]

A number of preliminary steps have already been taken. For example, a government-supported campaign has been launched in both regions to organize the unorganized segments of the labor force. At the next level, efforts are being made to unite existing organized labor within each region of the UAR in an all-embracing regional federation. In the Syrian region, the Confederation of Trade Unions has recently accomplished this goal. It currently comprises all of the general and industrial federations.[23] The Egyptian Confederation of Labor has also made considerable progress in this direction. Apparently there will be only one general confederation of labor in the UAR, with a separate general labor federation in each region.

In the meantime, a joint committee has drafted unified labor legislation for the United Arab Republic. The draft incorporates the best of both the Syrian and Egyptian labor legislation. In addition, it also relies heavily upon the ILO Conventions and Recommendations and the work of the Arab League Committee on Labor Legislation. Therefore, the unified labor legislation will represent in effect a revision and improvement of both region's labor legislation. Parts of the unified labor law have already been promulgated.

Finally, as a part of the bargain the ties of the Syrian labor movement to the WFTU had to be severed. The Communists were able to wrest control of several trade unions from the previously dominant Socialists during the period of close rapport between Syria and the USSR.[24] The strong influence of the Communists was reflected in open cooperation of the Syrian trade unions with the WFTU.[25] Under the UAR, however, Communism has been outlawed again in Syria. Moreover, the Syrian trade unions have expelled Communists from among their ranks.

On their part, the Egyptians were also forced to make a concession for the sake of a merger: complete severance of ties to Western labor organizations. The Syrian Petroleum Workers' Federation, for example, reportedly demanded the withdrawal of the Egyptian Chemical and Petroleum Workers' Federation from the ICFTU-affiliated International Federation of Petroleum Workers as a condition for their participation in an Arab petroleum federation.*

* Author's note: In the meantime, the Egyptian petroleum federation has

The Effects of Union upon Labor

Syrian labor had played a key role in the establishment of the International Confederation of Arab Trade Unions. Its first congress, for example, had been held in Syria, and its first president was a Syrian, Subhi al-Khatib. In addition, another Syrian was elected assistant secretary general. Under present arrangements, Syria retains four places on the executive council of the ICATU. In recent elections, however, Syrian labor won only the office of assistant secretary general. It appears that in the UAR, the southern region will play the dominant role in the ICATU.

In the United Arab Republic, Syrian labor faces stricter control and supervision over its affairs than it had under the independent Syrian governments. Its activities in the field of international labor are now controlled. Its only international trade union affiliation at present is the International Confederation of Arab Trade Unions. Moreover, foreign junkets of trade unionists must now get prior clearance from the government. In addition, in line with the attitude of the Egyptian government on strikes, the present Syrian Minister of Labor and Social Affairs stated that he "did not wish to hear of strikes or instances in which workers resort to striking." [26]

Nevertheless, things are not as black as they might appear. In fact, it appears that Syrian labor will enjoy generous treatment in the United Arab Republic. There is probably no Arab country, for example, that can match Egypt in the comprehensiveness or in the high quality of its labor and social legislation. Moreover, Egypt is currently vigorously enforcing it. It is generally agreed, therefore, that Syrian labor will gain substantially from unified social and labor legislation.

To be sure, Syrian labor will tend to lose its individuality and separate voice in international labor circles. But by the same token, the united labor movements of the UAR should gain increased prestige and importance in international circles.

JORDAN

In November 1954, Hallsworth wrote that no established trade union movement existed in Jordan.[27] Within a very short time,

re-established its association with the IFPW after an alienation which was never accepted as final by the IFPW.

however, a thriving labor movement had mushroomed into existence in Jordan. As a matter of fact, in 1955–56, the Federation of Trade Unions in Jordan was one of the most active crusaders for the establishment of the International Confederation of Arab Trade Unions.

The Jordanian labor movement, however, was not created *de novo*. It finds its roots in the Palestinian Arab labor movement which had existed prior to the partition of Palestine. The east bank of the Jordan (formerly Transjordan), however, had had no labor unions prior to its unification with Palestine. This is explained for the most part by the fact that industry had been practically non-existent on the east bank prior to the immigration of the Palestinian refugees. Roughly 80 per cent of the population of 1,500,000 inhabitants work and live on the land. The Labor Department announced, however, that in 1957 there were 17,051 industrial and commercial establishments employing 48,103 persons.[28]

Trade Union Development and Organization[29]

On 18 March 1950, remnants of the former Palestinian labor movement on the west bank of the Jordan River decided at a meeting held in Jericho to establish trade unions on the east bank. In effect, this marks the beginning of the labor movement in the Hashemite Kingdom of Jordan as a whole. When the movement succeeded in opening an office in Amman in 1952, however, the government promptly closed it on the ground that the current laws did not provide for unions. The earlier Transjordanian government had had no need to promulgate trade union legislation, and the present unified government had not yet gotten around to it.

In the meantime, however, trade unions on the west bank had been allowed under legislation enacted by the former Palestine government. Nevertheless, concurrently with its closure of the office in Amman, the government also clamped down on the trade unions on the west bank, apparently because of Communist infiltration. In 1953, however, the government promulgated new legislation legalizing trade unions in the entire kingdom.[30]

Labor responded quickly to the new provisions. As of the end of March 1957, a total of ninety organizations had applied for registration. Fifty had been registered as bona fide trade unions. Ten of these had their registrations canceled later, however, because they "deviated from the stated aims of their constitutions, or because they violated regulations of the Trade Union Law No. 35 of 1953." For example, six government employee unions were de-registered because their members did not qualify as "workers" under the law. As of 31 March 1957, there were forty registered trade unions with a total membership of 11,831 members.

TABLE 5. REGISTERED TRADE UNIONS IN JORDAN

YEAR	APPLICATIONS	REJECTIONS	REGISTRATION	CANCELLATIONS	REGISTERED UNIONS
1953/54	31	24	7	..	7
1954/55	32	14	18	..	18
1955/56	15	1	14	7	7
1956/57	12	1	11	3	8
Total	90	40	50	10	40

Source: The Hashemite Kingdom of Jordan, Ministry of Social Affairs, *Report on the Activities of the Ministry for the Year 1956/57* (in Arabic; Amman: Government Press, n.d.).

In the meantime, the Federation of Trade Unions in Jordan had been established and officially registered on 25 July 1954. Kharis and al-Safadi reported that twenty-five of the thirty-seven registered trade unions were affiliated to the federation at the end of 1955. At the end of March 1958, however, the federation claimed only eighteen affiliated unions. According to the federation's secretary general, these represented all of the registered and active unions in Jordan, with the exception of one unaffiliated union.[31]

RELATIONS WITH THE ICATU

Zaidan Yunus, the secretary of the Federation of Trade Unions in Jordan, was a moving spirit in the early stages of the pan-Arab labor movement. Under his leadership, the Jordanian federation became a founding member of the ICATU. Zaidan Yunus himself was elected assistant secretary general. Following the clash between King Husain and the Nabulsi government in April 1957, however, the labor movement came under close surveillance of the government. At the same time, the government dissolved parliament and the political parties and moved against the Communists and pro-Nasir elements. A number of both either fled the country or were jailed. Zaidan Yunus sought asylum in Syria.

It was reported at the time that the government had banned the trade union movement. In actual fact, however, the government had only suspended some of the unions whose leaders were involved in politics, contrary to union by-laws. By March 1958, the government had lifted all the suspensions, with one exception, and had allowed the unions to resume their normal activities. On 5 May 1957, however, the military governor had defined what these "normal activities" were henceforth to be:

> [The Military Governor] has assured us that the government is looking after labor affairs. It sincerely wants to give labor all its rights and to help the trade unions perform their complete task on behalf of labor. He further stated that the labor movement is designed solely for the good of labor, and is to be kept completely separate from political parties and politics. Its only objective is to raise the standard of the worker and to make him a useful member of society.[32]

In consequence, the government severed the close relations existing between the ICATU and organized labor in Jordan. Participation in the ICATU's activities has ceased, therefore, except on the part of expatriates like Zaidan Yunus, who is a member of the ICATU's executive council. Nevertheless, the ICATU has left the door open for the renewal of the old relationship and is keeping two additional places open on its executive council for Jordan.

LEBANON

Beirut, the capital of Lebanon, serves as an important entrepôt for goods destined for Syria, Jordan, and the Arabian peninsula. Therefore, most of Lebanon's non-agricultural labor force are employed in commerce. Nevertheless, Lebanon is rapidly developing industrially. The industrial census of 1955, for example, listed 1861 industrial establishments employing 35,013 workers. Of these, one hundred establishments employed more than fifty persons, and forty had more than a hundred employees.[33]

Trade Union Development and Organization[34]

Under the Free French and British occupation during World War II, the Lebanese labor movement made significant progress. By the time the labor code was promulgated in 1946, there were two "federations" in existence. One was the Communist-controlled

Federation of Unions of Workers and Employees under the presidency of the well-known Communist Mustafa al-'Aris. The other was an opposition group united together in the "Labor Front." Upon the promulgation of the labor code,[35] these and all other labor organizations were to apply for proper licenses.

The Communist-controlled federation refused to register, however, but has continued to function "illegally" to the present time. In the meantime, the League of Unions of Workers and Employees was established in 1946. It remained the only authorized federation until 1952, when a splinter group left it to form another federation. Currently, there are four registered federations to which most of the unions are affiliated. The combined union membership is between twenty and twenty-five thousand members.

On 30 April 1958, shortly before the Lebanese revolution broke out, the Minister of Social Affairs authorized the establishment of a general confederation of trade unions. The projected confederation, however, was not an all-inclusive body, for it comprised only three of the four authorized federations, not to mention the Communist-dominated federation. Before the founding members could elect officers, however, fighting had broken out. The actual establishment of the federation, therefore, was postponed. In March 1959, representatives of the three founding federations met to set up the basic organization and to consider the affiliation of the fourth authorized federation. Apparently, it had not been admitted initially because of personal differences among the labor leaders. The last preparatory meeting, before a general congress and elections, was scheduled on 24 March 1959.[36]

International Affiliations

The Communists have been involved in Lebanese labor affairs since the 1920's. In fact, they were responsible in large measure for the development of the Lebanese labor movement in its early stages. Therefore, when international labor got going again after the war, Mustafa al-'Aris was a delegate at the founding congress of the World Federation of Trade Unions in Paris in 1945. Moreover, he was elected a member of its executive committee for the Middle East. In the meantime, the WFTU came under Communist domination and Beirut became a strategic center for Communist activities in the Middle East. As a minor but important example of their activities, the WFTU located the publication office for the Arabic edition of the WFTU's monthly organ in Beirut.

To be sure, there are Communist trade unionists outside the federation of Mustafa al-'Aris. Nevertheless, the Lebanese Federation of Labor Unions itself has continued from his day to the present as the only active Lebanese affiliate of the WFTU. The head of the Lebanese Federation of Trade Unions is currently a member of the WFTU's executive committee, one of the vice-presidents is a regular member of the WFTU's general council, and another is a deputy member.

In the meantime, an opposing group, the League of Unions, affiliated itself to the anti-Communist International Confederation of Free Trade Unions at its founding congress in 1949. Currently the League is represented on the ICFTU's executive board. In addition, the independent oil unions in IPC and the Mobil Oil Company work with the anti-Communist International Federation of Petroleum Workers (IFPW). The ICFTU had set up a regional representative in Beirut in 1955 but he resigned after a short time. Meanwhile, the League of Unions' delegate to the ICFTU's congress in Tunis in 1957 asked for funds to combat the propaganda efforts of the WFTU in the area.

Relations with the ICATU

Two Lebanese federations became founding members of the International Confederation of Arab Trade Unions in 1956. In addition, representatives of the illegal Communist-dominated Lebanese federation participated in the early meetings, but were later barred except as observers because of their formal affiliation to the WFTU. Representatives of the League of Unions also took part in preliminary meetings and apparently pledged the support of the League to the ICATU. Upon returning to Beirut, however, they were ousted from office and the League rescinded its support. Unsuccessful bids had also been made to align the influential Association of IPC Employees and Workers with the new movement.

Several conflicting factors immediately came into focus on the issue of the ICATU. The fact that pan-Arabism is closely linked to Islam, for example, makes it less appealing to Lebanese Christian workers than to Moslems.[37] The pro-Western Lebanese labor organizations, of course, also tended to stay clear of the Egyptian-sponsored pan-Arab labor movement.[38]

With the exception of the Communists, Lebanese labor apparently acted with restraint during the civil disturbances in 1958. The ICATU had affirmed in May 1958 that it would not stand by with folded arms in the event of Western intervention in Lebanon.[39] The protagonists of the proposed Lebanese confederation, however, denounced the ICATU's call for volunteers and a collection of money to aid the "free people of Lebanon" in their struggle. Likewise, the other independent legal federation, the Federation of Allied Independent Unions (an affiliate of the ICATU), also protested against the interference of Syrian labor unions in Lebanon's affairs, when they offered contributions for the victims of fighting in Lebanon.[40]

Following the cessation of Lebanese hostilities, however, the problem of affiliation in the International Confederation of Arab Trade Unions came to the fore again. In the early stages of national recovery, for example, the Federation of Allied Independent Unions reportedly complained to the Lebanese President against being subjected to pressures from various quarters because of affiliation to the ICATU.[41] It was also reported that some advocates of a Lebanese confederation were considering withdrawing their endorsement and joining the ICATU.[42]

In the meantime, however, things have settled down to the normal Lebanese pattern of uneasy truce. The nascent confederation has agreed to accept into membership any labor organization, provided it is licensed by the government and is not involved in politics. Apparently this does not restrict member organizations from affiliating with either the ICFTU or the ICATU.[43] Nevertheless, the Lebanese confederation itself has indicated that it will not affiliate with any international trade union organization.

LIBYA

Libya is a vast "dust bowl" in which roughly 80 per cent of the million-plus population scratch a living from the land, half of them as nomads or semi-nomads. One observer has characterized Libya as "an example of universal poverty in extreme form." [44] Nevertheless, the industrial census conducted in 1956 indicated there were 13,690 industrial establishments employing 67,704 persons, or an average of roughly five persons per establishment.[45] Most of these are concentrated in the two cities of

Tripoli and Benghazi. Recent discoveries of petroleum reserves will undoubtedly bring many changes.

Trade Union Development and Organization [46]

Provincial legislation enacted in Tripolitania and Cyrenaica in 1951 granted legal recognition to trade unions.[47] Thereupon the Libyan General Workers' Union (LGWU) was formed, which is the largest and most important trade union organization in Libya. It has claimed 30,000 members on its rolls, but only about 4,000 are dues-paying members. It is organized as a large union with a number of sections but only one set of officers. Salim Shita is the president of the LGWU.

In addition, there are several independent unions. Two of the most important are the port workers' unions in Benghazi and Tripoli, the latter being especially well-disciplined and largely non-political. On 31 May 1958 the Libyan Petroleum Workers' Trade Union was registered. In view of the developing petroleum industry, this union promises to become of some importance in Libyan affairs. Within a few months of its establishment, the new union claimed 800 members and was already a recognized force in the Libyan labor movement. It is also organized as a unit (much like the LGWU), without separate unions in the various oil companies.

Relations with the ICFTU

Significantly, shortly after the establishment of the Petroleum Workers' Trade Union, a representative of the anti-Communist International Federation of Petroleum Workers (IFPW) visited Libya. A few months later, the IFPW announced that it had received the application of the Libyan petroleum union for affiliation. This action was not unusual, however, for the year the Libyan LGWU was established it had become an affiliate of the anti-Communist International Confederation of Free Trade Unions. In fact, North Africa has been one of the strongest supporters of the ICFTU in Africa as a whole.

In the meantime, the African Regional Organization of the ICFTU has been established, within which are three area committees. The North Africa area committee comprises Libya, Tunisia, Algeria, and Morocco. Labor leaders of these countries have held a number of joint meetings for the purpose of establishing a North African labor federation within the framework of the International Confederation of Free Trade Unions.

Relations with the ICATU

In his capacity as president of the Libyan General Workers' Union, Salim Shita has received a number of responsible assignments. For example, he has been the workers' representative to the International Labour Conference in Geneva and has been a substitute member of the ICFTU's executive board. In addition, he has been a member of the Tripolitanian Legislative Assembly. His most recent honor, however, was his election to the presidency of the International Confederation of Arab Trade Unions during its second congress held in Cairo in April 1959.

Salim Shita and Rajab al-Nayhum attended ICATU's founding congress in 1956 and were elected vice-president and assistant secretary general respectively. The Libyan General Workers' Union became a founding member of the ICATU. Rajab al-Nayhum, however, is head of an independent labor organization, the General Assembly of Cyrenaican Labor Unions. Reports indicated that he was refused permission to attend the meeting of ICATU's assistant secretaries general held in Cairo in September 1958. Apparently he also failed to attend the second congress.

The LGWU had the unique distinction of being an affiliate of both the ICATU and the ICFTU, which have been at odds with each other.* Its support of the ICFTU is due to its stands on North African independence, free trade unionism, and Communism. The ICATU, however, represents Arab nationalism. Nevertheless, Salim Shita had previously expressed serious misgivings about the close relations maintained between the ICATU and the Communist-dominated WFTU. The recent ban on Communist activities in the UAR, however, apparently has removed this objection.

THE SUDAN

The population of the Sudan is divided, broadly speaking, between the negroid tribal groups in the south and the Arabs in the north. The latter are much more advanced economically and culturally than the people of the southern provinces. Neverthe-

* Author's note: Reportedly the Adenese labor movement now also possesses this same distinction.

less, industrialization is still in its early stages in all the Sudan. More than 80 per cent of the Sudan's population of 10,262,500 depend on the land or water for their livelihood.[48] The British Labor Party government hopefully introduced trade unions into this society in 1946.

Trade Union Development and Organization [49]

In 1948 the Trade Unions Ordinance was promulgated. After its initial suspicion of the law had been dispelled, labor's response was rapid. Naturally, the number of trade unions is limited by the Sudan's underdeveloped economy. Nevertheless, by August 1957 the total number of registered trade unions was 157.[50] Their membership had been estimated at 55,000 members, from a non-agricultural labor force of about 210,000 persons. The most influential union was the Sudan Railway Workers' Union which claimed 20,106 members in 1956.

In 1950, the Sudan Workers' Trade Union Federation (SWTUF) was established to which most of the trade unions became affiliated. For some time, it was the only centralized labor organization in the Sudan. In April 1956, however, the Sudan Railway Workers' Union together with several other government workers' unions broke away from the SWTUF and set up a rival federation of their own. It claimed more than 24,000 members, its largest affiliate being the Sudan Railway Workers' Union.

Communist Infiltration

From the beginning, Communism has played a dominant role in the SWTUF. Early in its history, for example, its leaders had joined efforts with the Communist-dominated World Federation of Trade Unions to bring about a formal affiliation. Because of governmental restrictions in the Sudan, however, the SWTUF was forced into covert membership in the WFTU.[51] Nevertheless, al-Shafi' Ahmad al-Shaykh, secretary general of the SWTUF, was elected vice-president of the WFTU during its Fourth World Congress in Leipzig in 1957.

In early 1956, however, anti-Communists gained control for the first time of the large Railway Workers' Union and led the breakaway from the SWTUF. With encouragement from the government, they then set up the Sudan Government Workers' Trade Union Federation (SGWTUF) which, in turn, established relations with the anti-Communist International Confederation of Free Trade Unions. Three members of the SGWTUF, for example, attended the ICFTU's Regional Conference held in Accra in January 1957. In March 1958, therefore, the ICFTU approved the SGWTUF's application for affiliation. In the meantime, however, by devious means the Communists apparently had recaptured the largest part of the SGWTUF's membership and were again in command of the bulk of organized labor in the Sudan.[52]

Relations with the ICATU

In May 1957, the executive council of the International Confederation of Arab Trade Unions approved the application of the SWTUF for affiliation. Al-Shafi' Ahmad al-Shaykh became a member of the council.[53] By this act, the ICATU was able to boast of its broad-mindedness. On the one hand, through the Sudan's affiliation, the ICATU was associated with the WFTU; on the other hand, through Libya's affiliation, it was linked to the rival International Confederation of Free Trade Unions.

In the meantime, the SWTUF became one of the strong supporters of the ICATU. Even prior to formal affiliation, however, the SWTUF had responded to the decisions of the ICATU's executive council. In 1956, for example, in response to the ICATU's decision, the SWTUF called a two-hour general strike on behalf of Algeria. Then during the Suez Canal crisis, labor affiliates of the SWTUF refused to cooperate with the British and French civilian airlines passing through the Sudan. The SWTUF later played an important part in the Egyptian-sponsored Afro-Asian conferences. Shafi' al-Shaykh, for example, was granted a place on the three-member provisional secretariat of the International Trade Union Committee for Solidarity with the Workers and People of Algeria.

Government Crackdown

When the Sudan Workers' Trade Union Federation was established in 1950, there were no legal provisions made for federations. Nevertheless, by the same token federations per se were not illegal. The SWTUF, therefore, continued to function without specific legislation until 1957. Then an amendment specifically covering federations was made to the Trade Unions Ordinance of 1948. Of particular importance, the amendment stipulated registration. This requirement, while unknown in the United States and Britain, is a common device in the Arab world (and elsewhere) to insure government control over trade union business and finances. Moreover, the intent of registration is to enable the government to check that union activities are following lines acceptable to the government.

The SWTUF, however, refused to register. In addition, despite public notice by the labor registrar that the meeting would be illegal, the SWTUF openly held its Fifth General Conference in Khartoum in 1958. Therefore, the Sudanese government announced that it would not henceforth deal with the SWTUF, who represented a number of government workers' unions. Finally, in December 1958, following the peaceful coup d'état the government suspended the Communist-dominated trade unions "as a security measure." The leaders of the SWTUF were held and later given sentences of up to five years in jail.

Despite protests from the ICATU and the WFTU, the government continues to maintain a firm hand over labor. Therefore, its activities are in effect at a standstill and its relations with the ICATU have been cut off. An official delegation from the SWTUF, for example, was not able to attend the second congress of the ICATU in Cairo. Nevertheless, the ICATU has hopefully left three places open on its executive council for the Sudan Workers' Trade Union Federation.

CONCLUSION

In some areas the International Confederation of Arab Trade Unions has made considerable progress since 1956; in others it has suffered setbacks. The ICATU's membership and representation in the United Arab Republic, of course, have grown with the creation of an all-embracing labor organization in both regions of the UAR. Moreover, all "foreign" labor ties have been severed with the WFTU and the ICFTU, leaving the labor movements in the United Arab Republic entirely to the ICATU.

Elsewhere, the success of the ICATU has been, generally speaking, directly related to the relations existing between the UAR and the respective governments. The ICATU has suffered a setback, for example, in Jordan and Sudan where labor movements have been placed under government surveillance for their political activities. Moreover, both governments have encouraged labor contacts with the West. In fact, the ICFTU gained an affiliate in the Sudan. When friendlier relations are established between the respective Arab governments, however, relations between labor and the ICATU will probably also be resumed.

In the meantime, the creation of a general confederation of labor in Lebanon apparently will tend to exercise some restraint over its affiliates, in the direction of neutrality. The dominant organizations in the confederation are the League of Unions and the Federation of United Unions, both of which are generally opposed to the ICATU. In effect, this means no further increase in ICATU strength in Lebanon; there is the strong possibility of a loss.

Nevertheless, the fact that Communists have been cleaned out of the labor movement in the UAR has resolved misgivings which some had about the ICATU. In fact, the election of Salim Shita, president of the ICFTU-affiliated LGWU in Libya, is indicative of the anti-Communist line presently being taken by the pan-Arab labor movement. Nevertheless, this does not mean that the ICATU will become pro-West. On the contrary, it means that it has become more pro-Arab.

V

THE MISSION OF THE PAN-ARAB LABOR MOVEMENT IN THE ARAB WORLD

The Egyptian-backed pan-Arab labor movement apparently intends to follow President 'Abd al-Nasir's well-known theory of the three circles.[1] Accordingly, the International Confederation of Arab Trade Unions is to play a leading role in the Arab states from the Persian Gulf to the Atlantic, in Africa, and in the vast Muslim world extending through Asia and Africa. An Afro-Asian labor federation, of course, is an important element in the plans of the movement.

Initially, therefore, the pan-Arab labor movement established a regional federation. At its founding it comprised members from five Arab states. The next logical step was to expand the movement's affiliations to include all of the member states in the Arab League. After three years, however, the movement has added only one affiliate, the Sudanese SWTUF.[2] Nevertheless, the ICATU has had numerous contacts with the other labor movements. In some cases, it has enjoyed their active cooperation; in others, it has made significant contributions to their development.

From its epicenter in Cairo, the pan-Arab labor movement is seeking to expand to the Maghreb in the west, and to the oil-producing states in the east. The problems the International Confederation of Arab Trade Unions encounters are quite different in each area. On the one hand, trade unions are legal in North Africa and labor is well organized. On the other hand, unions have been illegal or suppressed in the other states and labor remains generally unorganized.

The brief treatment below of the ICATU's missionary activities will follow this natural division. Only limited historical background material will be introduced, as it serves the main purpose of tracing the pan-Arab labor movement.

THE MAGHREB

The largest and best organized labor movements in the Arab world are located in North Africa. They are closely tied to political parties, except in Libya where political parties are forbidden. In the international field, all of the North African labor movements are affiliated with the anti-Communist International Confederation of Free Trade Unions, with the exception of a few minor organizations. As a matter of fact, the bulk of the ICFTU's African membership is located in North Africa.

In the meantime, the International Confederation of Arab Trade Unions has concentrated considerable effort in this area. The winning of North Africa's affiliation as a bloc, of course, would represent a major step forward in both its Arab and African programs. Up to the present time, however, only the Libyan labor movement has formally affiliated with the ICATU. Nevertheless, Libya's example demonstrates the possibility of joint affiliations in both the ICATU and the ICFTU. Significantly, the current president of the ICATU is a North African, the head of the Libyan ICFTU-affiliated LGWU.

TUNISIA

The *Union Générale Tunisienne du Travail* (UGTT) is the all-embracing labor movement in Tunisia.[3] Estimates of its membership run as high as 225,000 members.[4] By virtue of Tunisia's former relationship to France, the early development of the Tunisian movement had been perforce tied to the French metropolitan *Confédération Générale du Travail* (CGT). When the Tunisian movement espoused nationalism, however, it split from the CGT. The UGTT was established as an autonomous organization on 20 January 1946.[5]

In the meantime, another smaller group had also broken away from the CGT. Like the UGTT, the *Union des Syndicats des Travailleurs de Tunisie* (USTT) had taken on nationalist trappings. On this basis, the Communist-dominated USTT sought reunification with the UGTT, but without success. Finally in 1956 the USTT dissolved itself and its members sought admission on an individual basis in the UGTT. Those who were admitted did so on probation.

To be sure, the UGTT itself had been admitted into the World

Federation of Trade Unions in 1949 but followed the lead of the other non-Communist organizations shortly thereafter and renounced its affiliation. In 1951, the UGTT joined the International Confederation of Free Trade Unions, and their relations since have been close. The ICFTU gave strong support to the Tunisian independence movement; the UGTT in turn became one of the ICFTU's strongest African supporters. Ahmad Talili, the secretary general of the UGTT, is currently a member of the ICFTU's executive board. The ICFTU itself held its Fifth World Congress in Tunis in 1957, the first time it had been held outside Europe.

The nationalist struggle for independence from France had brought the UGTT into a close alliance with the Neo-Destour, the party of President Bourguiba. Close interlocking relations on the executive level bind the two organizations together. The achievement of independence, however, has sometimes strained the common bond between the two organizations, for their interests are not always identical. This was revealed in the split which took place in the UGTT in 1956, out of which a splinter group grew and existed for a short time as the *Union Tunisienne du Travail* (UTT).

By virtue of this rupture, the International Confederation of Arab Trade Unions felt that its star had indeed risen in Tunisia. For under the leadership of the UGTT, the Tunisian labor movement had remained aloof from the blandishments of the ICATU. A delegation from the ICATU, for example, attended the UGTT's Sixth General Congress in September 1956 but apparently made no progress in winning the leaders over to the ICATU. However, the inherent possibilities of a rival movement made the ICATU optimistic.[6]

Nothing came of this, however, for the Tunisian labor movement was soon reunited. Moreover, the split and reunion were apparently a maneuver of internal politics to bring the UGTT into line with the government's leadership.[7] Therefore, a rapprochement between the Tunisian labor movement and the Egyptian-backed ICATU remains unlikely, in view of current strained relations between the two governments.

While the UGTT has publicly come to the defense of the pan-Arab labor movement against an outside attack, it nevertheless feels that the ICATU is essentially a misguided movement: [8]

Our duty and our task must consist either of convincing the leaders of this Federation [viz., the ICATU] in order to bring them back on to the right lines, or to make efforts to organize and to group the workers of this region in free trade unions which will take us as a model for their work and which will join our International. We must achieve this by making use of all the available energy and good will . . . .[9]

Morocco

The *Union Marocaine du Travail* (UMT) is the all-embracing trade union organization of Morocco.[10] It was formally established on 20 March 1955 during the struggle for national independence, and was closely allied with the Istiqlal Party in this common effort. In fact, joining the UMT at this time was a manifestation of nationalism, without the social or economic connotations normally associated with trade union membership.

The French authorities had refused to recognize autonomous Moroccan unions. Instead, the Moroccan workers (like the Tunisians) had been forced to join the Communist-dominated CGT. Therefore, a number of the present leaders of both movements got their early trade union schooling in the CGT. Nevertheless, both movements turned to the anti-Communist International Confederation of Free Trade Unions which, in turn, gave them strong support in their nationalist independence movements. The UMT claims 880,000 members.[11]

While the UMT has retained its membership, it wants broader contacts than are represented in the ICFTU. On this basis, the UMT has maintained fraternal relations with labor movements in Communist countries. Moreover, the UMT refuses to follow the straight ICFTU line. For example, the UMT has on occasion opposed stands endorsed by the ICFTU at the ILO conferences in Geneva. The UMT also refused to participate in the ICFTU-sponsored African Regional Conference held in Accra in 1957.

The UMT's secretary general, Mahjub ibn al-Sadiq, provided the reasons for their failure to participate in this conference in a speech which he delivered a few months later in Tunis before the fifth congress of the ICFTU. One reason he gave was of particular interest, in view of the Afro-Asian and pan-African movements:

In Africa the problem of unity and the problem of freedom take precedence over any other conflict of an ideological nature. We are not at all anxious to divide the African workers on ideological bases [viz., ICFTU vs. ICATU or WFTU, etc.] . . . In our view, therefore, our first task is the unification of the African continent and of the African workers.[12]

In the meantime, the UMT established cordial relations with the International Confederation of Arab Trade Unions. Its secretary general, Fathi Kamil, for example, was invited to attend the UMT's May Day celebrations in 1957. Then at the ICFTU's Fifth World Congress held in Tunis in 1957, the UMT's secretary general al-Mahjub ibn al-Sadiq protested "energetically against the gratuitous attack" which the ICFTU's secretary general had leveled against the ICATU.[13] In November of the same year, al-Mahjub ibn al-Sadiq and Fathi Kamil issued a joint communiqué during another visit of the latter to Morocco:

> The two parties resolve to redouble their efforts to strengthen the fraternal ties between them; to reinforce the bonds of struggle for the liberation of the countries which still sink under the rule of imperialist; to augment liaison for the ready exchange of views; and to coordinate efforts for the achieving of everything that will assure workers in the Arab world of a life of freedom, justice, and creature comforts.[14]

In the spring of 1958, al-Mahjub ibn al-Sadiq visited the United Arab Republic. Again the two secretaries general issued a joint communiqué. In it they endorsed (*inter alia*) the recommendations of the Afro-Asian Peoples' Solidarity Conference which had been held in Cairo the previous December.[15] The UMT had also participated in the Cairo-sponsored International Trade Union Conference for the Victory of the Workers and People of Algeria, which was held in September 1958 in Cairo. Representatives of the UMT, the ICATU, and the WFTU were chosen to comprise a three-member provisional secretariat for the conference.[16]

On the basis of these close fraternal relations, the ICATU has entertained hopes that the UMT would seek affiliation. Available evidence indicates, however, that while the UMT has strong pan-Arab tendencies it will not affiliate at present with the ICATU. Nevertheless, the ICATU executive decided in September 1958 to facilitate cooperation with non-member Arab labor organizations by inviting them to attend its second congress as observers.[17] The UMT attended the congress on this basis, as did labor organizations from other Arab states.

Algeria

In 1956, the *Union Générale des Syndicats Algériens* (UGSA) was established as an autonomous national trade union federation directly affiliated to the WFTU. The UGSA has a claimed membership of 5000 members. A much larger group, however, had also broken away from the Algerian CGT organization and had established the *Union Générale des Travailleurs Algériens* (UGTA). It claims 150,000 members and is affiliated to the ICFTU. In the meantime, the *Union des Syndicats des Travailleurs Algériens* (USTA) had also been established. It claims a membership of 50,000, most of whom work in metropolitan France.[18]

The French authorities alleged that the USTA and the UGTA represented nothing more than the labor arms of two nationalist political movements, the *Mouvement National Algérien* (MNA) and the *Front de Libération Nationale* (FLN), respectively. For this reason alone, the French government alleges, they have been banned.

The UGSA, however, had been a regional federation of the CGT and had enjoyed legal status by virtue of that relationship until it split from the CGT. The moment it became an autonomous movement, the UGSA automatically lost its legal status. At the same moment it had allegedly taken on an essentially political character. Like the others it too was banned. In general, therefore, the trade union activities per se of all these organizations have ceased.

The International Confederation of Free Trade Unions has championed the Algerian cause, as it had done for Tunisia and Morocco earlier. It was not unusual, therefore, that the Algerian issue was the dominant theme of the ICFTU's fifth congress in Tunis in 1957. The ICFTU's position on the issue, in essence, calls for negotiations between the two parties, but based on recognition of the right of the Algerian people to self-determination.

The International Confederation of Arab Trade Unions, however, has also strongly supported the Algerian cause. In October 1956, for example, the ICATU called a general strike to protest the French kidnapping of the Algerian leaders. The following May, the ICATU invited Rashid 'Abd al-'Aziz of the UGTA to attend a meeting of the ICATU's executive council in Cairo. Perhaps the most dramatic effort of the ICATU, however, has been the International Trade Union Conference for the Victory of the Workers and People of Algeria, which was held in September 1958 in Cairo. Since the WFTU was a co-sponsor of the conference, the guest list of eighteen international organizations was oriented in that direction. A reunion of the group took place in May 1959 in Sofia, Bulgaria; four UGTA delegates attended.

Algerian delegates also participated as observers in the ICATU's second congress held in April 1959 in Cairo. The congress called upon Arabs to contribute materially and morally to the Algerian revolution, and to organize an "Algeria Week," as recommended by the Afro-Asian Peoples' Solidarity Conference.

Like the Moroccan labor movement, the Algerian movement's relations cover a broad spectrum. Its ultimate direction, however, cannot be determined until a settlement has been reached in Algeria and labor organizations are allowed to function freely. In the meantime, however, the ICATU is building up a good case for itself in the ranks of the Algerian labor movement.

North African Federation

The two fundamental objectives in North Africa at present are the independence of Algeria and the unification of the Maghreb. On these two points there is a basic community of purpose among the Istiqlal, the Neo-Destour, and the FLN. It is generally assumed that unification would follow Algerian independence.[19] In the meantime, however, their labor counterparts have been actively working toward unification of the North African trade union movements.

The International Confederation of Free Trade Unions has been closely associated with the idea of North African labor unity. In fact, the trade union leaders of North Africa held their first meeting on the subject in the ICFTU headquarters in Brussels in July 1956.[20] Therefore, when the ICFTU established its African Regional Organization in 1957, the North African labor leaders welcomed the decision. They intend to affiliate the united Maghreb center to it.[21] The North African federation would comprise one of the three area committees which have been provided in the ICFTU's African Regional Organization.

Apparently agreement had been reached in the meantime between the combined North African trade union leadership and the International Confederation of Arab Trade Unions to cooperate in their efforts for the liberation of Algeria. This may explain the heterogeneous character of the International Trade Union Conference for the Victory of the Workers and People of Algeria which was held in Cairo in 1958. On the one hand, the list [22] of countries represented at this conference included Algeria, Morocco, and Tunisia [23] — all ICFTU affiliates. On the other hand, the list included organizations from the USSR, the

Sudan, Red China, East Germany and others — all WFTU affiliates, plus four representatives of the WFTU itself. In between was the International Confederation of Arab Trade Unions.

Several factors make affiliation with the International Confederation of Arab Trade Unions more attractive today than two years ago; e.g., the "clamp down" on Communism in the UAR; the waning pro-Western feeling among North African labor;[24] and increasing pan-Arabism. Moreover, it has been pointed out that North African labor would have an unrivaled position as a bloc in the ICATU, such as it could never enjoy in the ICFTU. Nevertheless, by virtue of its preoccupation with the establishment of its own federation, there is little likelihood that North African labor, as a bloc, will go beyond the present stage of informal "fraternal relations."

THE OIL-PRODUCING STATES

Little more than a decade ago, trade union organizers passed over the states of the *Jazirat al-'Arab* with hardly a second glance. Today the international labor organizations are competing with each other in the area. Oil has made the difference. Not unnaturally, a conflict of interests has arisen between the International Confederation of Arab Trade Unions and the International Federation of Petroleum Workers (IFPW). More than 50,000 Arab petroleum workers are at stake.[25]

Delegations from these states appear from time to time at various international trade union conferences. On the whole they are "bogus delegations," for organized labor movements exist today only in Iraq and Aden. Nevertheless, significant progress has been made towards organizing labor in the general area. The ICATU, to a very large degree, has been responsible — as a catalytic agent.

Petroleum Workers

The International Federation of Petroleum Workers was established in 1954. Delegates from fifteen countries attended the founding conference in Paris. The organizing drive, however, came from the Oil Workers' International Union (CIO), now the Oil, Chemical, and Atomic Workers' International Union (AFL-CIO). Its president and international representative were elected president and general secretary, respectively, of the IFPW.

The IFPW has had relatively close relations with the Arab

world. Anwar Salamah, president of the Egyptian Petroleum and Chemical Workers' Federation, was elected a director of the IFPW at its founding conference.[26] At its second congress, which was held in Rome in July 1957, he was elected second vice-president by unanimous vote.[27]

The first resolution passed by this congress authorized the general secretary to establish an office in the Middle East, later announced to be located in Cairo. This precipitated considerable opposition from the pan-Arab labor movement. In fact, the Egyptian Petroleum Workers' Federation itself was finally forced to withdraw from the IFPW over this issue.[28]

Apparently as a counter move to the IFPW, it was announced on 27 December 1958 that an International Arab Federation of Oil and Chemical Workers had been established. Reportedly it comprised petroleum workers from the United Arab Republic, Iraq, and Aden. It appears, however, that this was only a meeting of a preparatory committee and that the delegates from Iraq and Aden were not bona fide representatives.

At any rate, such a federation had been proposed much earlier,[29] and Anwar Salamah had visited several Arab countries in quest of its establishment. The membership in the IFPW of the Egyptian federation itself, however, appears to have been the stumbling block. When this was removed the petroleum federation of Syria was ready to merge with its counterpart in the other region of the UAR, thereby paving the way for an international Arab federation of petroleum workers.[30]

The IFPW appears puzzled whether the new federation intends to replace it in the Arab world, or whether the new organization is to become a regional member of the IFPW. The IFPW hopes for the latter and has, therefore, sought to heal the rift between it and the Egyptian Petroleum Workers' Federation. In the meantime, however, the IFPW has been carrying on with its own organizing work in the area. In October 1958, for example, the IFPW announced the application of the Libyan Petroleum Workers' Trade Union for affiliation.[31]

Iraq. The population of Iraq was estimated to be somewhat more than 4,800,000 persons in 1955, excluding foreigners and nomadic tribes. Most of the population live and work on the land. The first Iraqi industrial census of 1955 showed 22,460 industrial establishments with a total employment of 90,291 persons. Only 294 of these establishments employed more than twenty persons.

The average size of the remaining 22,166 establishments was 2.3 persons.[32] The 1957 *Census of Services Industries*[33] indicated that there were 15,656 service establishments employing 48,878 persons. The small size of the average establishment is obvious.

This factor, of course, has hindered the development of trade unionism. Nevertheless, there are some relatively large establishments in Iraq. The 294 establishments with more than twenty employees, for example, had an average employment of 132 persons. The petroleum companies, the state railways, and the Basrah Port Authority are the largest employers, with 15,328, 14,256, and 7874 employees respectively.[34]

The chief factor responsible for the belated development of the Iraqi labor movement, however, had been the former conservative governments.[35] They appeared mortally afraid of trade unions.[36] To be sure, trade unions had been legalized as far back as 1936. Nevertheless, the government suppressed some for Communist activities, e.g., the Basrah Port and the Iraq railway workers' unions. On others it imposed severely restrictive controls. The petroleum workers remained unorganized. Therefore, prior to the July 14 Revolution of 1958, very few legal labor unions existed.

Nevertheless, the new Iraqi labor legislation reflects an element of progressive leadership within the Ministry of Social Affairs. In particular, the Labor Law of 1958 was indicative of a new approach to trade unions.[37] Apparently, the government itself intended to cultivate and develop the trade union movement, as Egypt had done.

Two days before the new labor law was to go into effect, the revolution removed the old regime. Nevertheless, the labor law became effective on schedule, except for the provisions dealing with trade unions. They were outlawed for the time being. Those which were established during this period were suspended, on the grounds that they were operating without proper authorization. Thereupon, "constituent" trade union organizations were established, in anticipation of the expected authorization. And in January 1959, the new government approved the issue of permits for the establishment of trade unions.

The announcement brought a flood of applications. The first permit was granted to the railway workers; another was granted the Basrah Port workers. During February, the government issued licenses to thirty-two unions. In the meantime, it has been reported that the petroleum workers have been organized in a central organization in Baghdad. Finally, establishment of a general confederation of labor has also been reported. Indeed, Iraqi labor has been organized on an unprecedented scale under the new regime.

Meanwhile, a number of Communist front organizations have been established. Apparently with very good reason, the secretary general of the Iraqi Peace Partisans links labor with these front organizations:

On the people's initiative, peasant societies and workers' trade unions, and such organizations as the Peace Movement, the Democratic Youth Movement, the Students' Union and the Women's Rights League, have been restored and are now actively participating in the country's life.[38]

The International Confederation of Arab Trade Unions had been cheered by the news of the Iraq revolution and entertained high hopes of another affiliate.[39] Therefore, when an Iraqi trade union movement failed to materialize as expected after the revolution, UAR labor made enquiries of the responsible Iraqi authorities.[40] In the meantime, however, pan-Arabism was on the wane in Iraq. Consequently, by the time legal trade unions were established, it seemed obvious that they would not join the pan-Arab ICATU. UAR sources referred to the Iraqi trade unions as Communist-controlled organizations.[41]

The earlier participation of Iraqi labor in the pan-Arab labor movement apparently had gone no further than unofficial representation at the ICATU's founding conference in Damascus in 1956.[42] It was not unusual, however, that pro-Nasir Iraqi labor leaders attended the ICATU's second congress held in Cairo in April 1959. As a matter of fact, the Iraqi situation and the Communist threat to the Arab world dominated the attention of the congress. Of particular interest, however, the ICATU accepted the affiliation at this congress of a "Confederation of Trade Unions in the Republic of Iraq," which claimed thirty central labor unions with outlying branches.

Supposedly it had existed as a clandestine organization prior to the 14 July Revolution and had been a secret affiliate of the ICATU. After the revolution, the movement emerged into the open under the name given above. Following the Mosul rebellion in March 1959, however, it is alleged that the movement was proscribed again and its leaders dispersed.[43]

Therefore, the ICATU's second congress resolved to send a cable of protest to the Iraqi government; declared an "Iraq Day" for soliciting donations for "bleeding Iraq;" and established a committee to gather information on the incidents occurring in Iraq. A protest was then to be made to the International Labour Office in Geneva.

In the meantime, however, Iraqi labor unions have protested against "unwarranted interference" from the International Confederation of Arab Trade Unions in their affairs.[44]

Bahrain.[45] According to the 1950 census,[46] Bahrain's population totaled 109,650 inhabitants. The 1956 *Census of Employment* divided the labor force as shown in Table 6.

TABLE 6. DISTRIBUTION OF BAHRAIN'S LABOR FORCE

INDUSTRY	NO. OF ESTABLISHMENTS	NO. OF PEOPLE EMPLOYED		TOTAL
		Bahrainis	*Foreigners*	
Manufacturing	687	716	996	1712
Construction	103	2492	1472	3964
Oil Industry	1	5826	2959	8785
Mining and Quarrying	3	49	17	66
Trade and Banking	2507	3368	2449	5817
Transport and Communications	57	887	864	1751
Services	443	4055	3446	7501
Total	3801	17,393	12,203	29,596
Estimated:				
Taxi and bus drivers				750
Maritime Industry				4000
Agriculture, domestic service, fishing				8000
Total Labor Force				42,346

Source: R. S. Porter, *Report on the Census of Employment in Bahrain 1956* (Beirut, 1957).

One of the striking features in Bahrain's employment pattern is the proportionately large foreign element. Roughly 41 per cent of those registered in the employment census were foreigners.[47] They have generated serious problems of labor relations,[48] and as a divisive element they have stood in the way of labor organization.

Bahrain's chronic Sunni-Shi'i differences were resolved in 1954 in a movement led by a self-styled Higher Executive Committee (HEC), composed of four Sunnis and four Shi'as. The HEC was the central steering group of a larger anonymous group of one hundred. Initially the movement aimed at reforms, but gradually the idea of reform gave way to plans for revolt. The leaders were ultimately sentenced to long prison terms and were banned to St. Helena, on charges of plotting against the government and planning the assassination of various members of the government.

A labor movement arose as a part of the general movement spearheaded by the HEC. Organizationally, the labor movement never got much beyond the constituent committee stage, before the government cracked down on the HEC in 1956.[49] Nevertheless, the "Bahrain Labor Federation" claimed 6000 members (all Bahrainis) in 1956. Despite eminently fair provisions in the new labor law [50] which went into effect on 1 January 1958, the labor movement has not recovered from the setback of 1956.

The International Confederation of Arab Trade Unions apparently played an active supporting role in the Bahrain labor movement in 1956. Quite certainly Egyptian influence was brought to bear upon the development of Bahrain's labor legislation.[51] The pan-Arab labor movement continues to be actively interested in Bahraini labor. The ICATU, for example, adopted the following resolution in the course of its second congress in 1959:

> The Congress recommends sending a remonstration to the Bahrain Government against the oppression of the trade-union movement, and demands the release of the free Bahraini Arabs who were detained and deported to the Island of St. Helena, during the Tripartite Aggression on Egypt.

Kuwait, Qatar, and Saudi Arabia. The local labor market in these states has been unable to supply the skills required in the oil industry or in the industries it has spawned. The very small populations of Qatar and Kuwait, of course, are important factors to account for this — about 35,000 and 250,000 inhabitants, respectively. The decisive factor in all cases, however, has been the very high illiteracy rate. Therefore Westerners, Indians and Pakistanis, and Levantine Arabs have been brought in to supply the missing skills.

Nevertheless, by 1957 roughly 70 per cent of the labor force of the Arabian American Oil Company were Saudi Arabs.[52] The oil companies in the other two states, however, have been less fortunate. Indeed, the industrial labor forces taken as a whole in Kuwait and Qatar are predominately foreign. Table 7, which was prepared by an Egyptian labor expert in Kuwait's Department of Social Affairs, is indicative at least of the extent of the foreign element in the labor force.

TABLE 7. RATIO OF FOREIGNERS TO KUWAITIS IN SPECIFIED VOCATIONS OR INDUSTRIES

VOCATION OR INDUSTRY	PERCENTAGE OF FOREIGN WORKERS
Hotels or Industry	95
Printing and Photography	92
Carpentry and Mechanical Work	99
Airlines, Tourism, and Travel	90
Electricity	92
Automotive Repairing	98
Security	83
Ocean Navigation	87

Source: Amin 'Izz al-Din, *Kuwait's Workers: From the Pearl to Petroleum* (in Arabic; Kuwait: Government Press, 1958), p. 10. These estimates seem on the high side. He did not indicate, for example, whether the figures included the employment of Kuwait Oil Company. If so, the figures would be high. Nevertheless, the author points out that at the end of 1957 there were 40,628 foreigners registered with the government. In addition, of course, there were many who had not bothered to register.

The large foreign element, of course, has produced innumerable problems of labor relations. In addition, from the workers' point of view, the heterogeneous character of the labor force precludes united action. Consequently, in these states, labor strikes which are often labeled "general" strikes, are general strikes only so far as the local Arab employees are concerned. The other nationalities usually remain on the job.

These states were without important industrial labor forces until the development of the petroleum industry. Therefore, they had no real need for labor legislation. Nevertheless, as early as 1937 Saudi Arabia enacted industrial compensation provisions,[53] which, in a series of subsequent steps, led to the Labor and Workman Regulations of 1947.[54] The other states, however, have remained without formal provisions for labor, except for government personnel.

There are no provisions for trade unions in these states, except to forbid them. Saudi Arabia has been no more severe in this regard than its neighbors, merely more explicit. Its anti-strike decree of 1956 aroused strong protests from international labor.[55] The decree effectively suppressed a nascent labor movement.

Attempts by the oil companies in the Persian Gulf at introducing communications or joint consultative committees in lieu of unions have in general also failed. Labor has adamantly refused to go along with what it considers a poor substitute for trade unions. On the other side of the coin, the ruler of Qatar apparently refused to allow the Qatar Petroleum Company to establish such committees because they might lead to trade unions.[56]

In the meantime, progressive Arab forces are at work in these states. For example, the Arab governments have brought in a number of Arab experts to assist in the fields of labor and social affairs. Saudi Arabia has had Egyptians assist its Labor Department and Royal Commission for Labor Affairs. Similarly in Kuwait, its Department of Social Affairs has had a number of Egyptian experts. Some were called in to draft a labor law, for example, which in its published draft form contains provisions for trade unions.[57]

In addition, a number of local Arabs have gone abroad for their higher education and have returned to government service. The present assistant director of the Department of Labor in Saudi Arabia, for example, was educated in Egyptian universities. A former director took his degree in Industrial Relations from the University of California. These men in general represent progressive elements in the labor field.

Labor leaders in the area sent messages of support to the founding congress of the pan-Arab labor movement in 1956. In turn, the International Confederation of Arab Trade Unions carried a relatively long article on Saudi Arabian labor conditions in the first issue of its official organ. Unofficial delegates from Saudi Arabia and Kuwait attended the second congress in 1959. It passed several resolutions relative to Saudi Arabia, calling for social and political reforms, freedom of association for labor, cancellation of "reactionary legislation," and the promulgation of more favorable labor legislation.

There were no specific resolutions issued relative to Kuwait. To be sure, it also has no trade unions.[58] Nevertheless, there are more promising prospects for trade unionism in Kuwait than in Saudi Arabia. While the ICATU representatives have been kept out of Arabia, for example, they have been allowed in Kuwait.[59] Moreover, Egyptian labor experts have been allowed to publish articles in defense of trade unionism in the Kuwait government's official publications.[60]

The currents of pan-Arabism run strong in the Persian Gulf states. If trade unions were allowed, there is a strong likelihood that they would attempt to affiliate with the International Confederation of Arab Trade Unions.

Aden Colony. Aden consists of a Crown Colony and Protectorates, together with certain islands. This section deals only with the Colony, which has a relatively large industrial labor force and an organized trade union movement. In 1955 the total population of the Colony was 138,441 inhabitants. Table 8 shows the distribution of the labor force as of the end of December 1957.

TABLE 8. EMPLOYMENT IN THE PRINCIPAL INDUSTRIES AND SERVICES OF ADEN

EMPLOYMENT	NUMBER OF EMPLOYEES
Port	7,517
Building and Construction	8,977
Industrial Undertakings	10,011
Retail and Wholesale Trade	4,265
Government and Other Services	4,906
Miscellaneous	433
Total	36,109

Source: Aden Colony, *Annual Report of the Department of Labour and Welfare*, 1956–1957 (Aden: Government Printer, n.d.), p. 60.

The first trade union was registered in 1952.[61] The movement did not get under way, however, until 1955 and later. At the end of 1957 there were twenty-seven worker organizations with a claimed membership of about 12,000 members. The number of dues-paying members, however, probably did not exceed 4500 members. In 1956 a Trade Union Congress (TUC) was established to which the majority of the registered unions are affiliated.[62]

The Aden TUC is affiliated with the International Confederation of Free Trade Unions. At its Fifth World Congress in 1957, the ICFTU elected the TUC's 'Abd Allah 'Ubaid a substitute member of its executive board. In the meantime, the ICFTU has supported the TUC in its stand against immigrating foreign workers (viz., Somalis, Indians, etc.), who compete with unemployed Adenese for jobs. Moreover, the ICFTU has supported a TUC complaint to the ILO against infringement of trade union rights in the Colony. The TUC in turn had a student at the first session in November 1958 of the ICFTU's new trade union training center in Kampala.

The International Confederation of Arab Trade Unions, however, has also been making a strong bid for the support of Adenese labor, with some success. The TUC, for example, sent delegates to the ICATU-sponsored international trade union conference in support of Algeria in September 1958. Then in December 1958 it was rumored (but without subsequent substantiation) that an International Arab Federation of Petroleum and Chemical Workers had been established and that Aden was a founding member. In April 1959, however, the Aden Trade Union Congress was represented at the second congress of the International Confederation of Arab Trade Unions in Cairo.

In 1959, the position had been described as a tug of war between the two internationals with the ICFTU holding the advantage at the moment. In the meantime, however, pan-Arabists were throwing a lot of water around its feet.[63] It has been reported recently that the Adenese labor movement has affiliated with the International Confederation of Arab Trade Unions. Thus Aden has joined Libya in possessing joint affiliations with the pan-Arab movement and the International Confederation of Free Trade Unions.

VI

POSITIVE NEUTRALITY AND ARAB LABOR

The activities of the newly-established International Confederation of Arab Trade Unions were bound to overlap those of the World Federation of Trade Unions and its counterpart, the anti-Communist International Confederation of Free Trade Unions. In fact, Arab affiliates of both the WFTU and the ICFTU attended the founding conference of the pan-Arab labor movement in Damascus in 1956. The possibilities for conflict, however, were far greater than for cooperation among the three or, for that matter, between any two of them.

THE SETTING FOR A STRUGGLE OVER ARAB LABOR

As indicated earlier, world labor had oriented itself on an East–West basis. Two giant international trade union movements had developed since World War II, the World Federation of Trade Unions and the International Confederation of Free Trade Unions. Both were competing in the uncommitted areas of the world for labor's support for their respective causes.

The first of these, the World Federation of Trade Unions, was established in October 1945 at a conference of trade union leaders in Paris.[1] It was attended by delegates from fifty-six countries, territories, and colonial areas, representing 67,000,000 organized workers. Its founders had many motives, of course, but all shared one common purpose — to bring world labor's influence to bear upon the making of the peace at the end of World War II and upon postwar reconstruction. This explains the unlikely coalition of the British Trades Union Congress (TUC) and the American Congress of Industrial Organizations (CIO) with the Communist-dominated French *Confédération Générale du Travail* (CGT) and the Soviet trade unions.

After a couple of years, however, these heterogeneous elements broke into two diametrically opposed camps, the free trade unions versus the Communist trade unions. Finally, in the early part of 1949 the CIO and the TUC with the Dutch affiliate withdrew entirely from the WFTU. They were joined later by the French *Force Ouvrière* (a splinter from the CGT) and other free trade unions. In December 1949 they established the International Confederation of Free Trade Unions. At its founding conference in London there were delegates from fifty-three countries, who claimed to represent 48,000,000 workers.[2]

Since then both the WFTU and the ICFTU have flourished, especially on their own home grounds.[3] It has been in the uncommitted "neutral" areas of the world, however, where they have faced their most difficult task in winning affiliates. In the Arab world, where both have been very active, the ICFTU has been far more successful than the WFTU in this regard, particularly in North Africa.

In the meantime, however, the new force of the International Confederation of Arab Trade Unions began to compete with them in this area in 1956. Their relative strength at the end of 1957 is shown in Table 9.

TABLE 9. INTERNATIONAL LABOR AFFILIATIONS IN THE ARAB WORLD

		Affiliated With				
Country	Total Union Membership	ICFTU	CISC [a]	WFTU	ICATU	Without Affiliation
Aden	11,511	9,305				2,206
Algeria	320,000	175,000	35,000	5,000		105,000
Egypt	275,000				275,000	
Iraq	821					821
Jordan	11,248				5,953	5,295
Lebanon	21,478	4,000		2,400	5,715	9,363
Libya [b]	5,000	4,000			4,000	1,000
Morocco	880,000	880,000				
Syria	32,213				32,213	
Sudan [c]	54,335	24,221		17,956	17,956	12,158
Tunisia	226,000	225,000	1,000			

Source: U.S. Department of Labor, Office of International Labor Affairs, *Directory of Labor Organizations, Africa*, and *Directory of Labor Organizations, Asia and Australasia* (Washington, 1958).

[a] *Confédération Internationale des Syndicats Chrétiens* (International Federation of Christian Trade Unions: often referred to as the IFCTU). Compared with the ICFTU and the WFTU, the CISC is a small organization. Its main strength is in France, Belgium, and Holland. It has consultative status as a Category A organization in the Economic and Social Council of the UN and in the ILO. (Cf. U.S. Department of Labor, Office of International Labor Affairs, *Directory of the International Federation of Christian Trade Unions* [CISC], 1955.)

[b] Four thousand members are shown in both the ICFTU and ICATU column, but not in the over-all total.

[c] The application of the Government Workers' Federation for membership in the ICFTU was approved in March 1958. In this respect, the table's figures differ from the source cited. There are 17,956 members shown in both the WFTU and ICATU column, but not in the over-all total.

To be sure, the pan-Arab labor movement could have concentrated its efforts on the unaffiliated trade union membership. Nevertheless, if the ICATU expected to expand to any extent at all, it would obviously have to do so at the expense of the ICFTU. The WFTU had no significant membership in the Arab world.

ARAB PARTICIPATION IN THE ICFTU

A number of Arab trade unionists had participated in the founding of the ICFTU in 1949.[4] Fathi Kamil, for example, of the Egyptian Tobacco Workers' Union and later president of the pan-Arab labor movement attended as an observer.

In addition, Ibrahim Zain al-Din of the General Union of Mechanics and Motor Drivers of Cairo was there. He became the Middle East representative on the general council of the International Transport Workers' Federation (ITF), an International Trade Secretariat (ITS). In 1954, the International Federation of Petroleum Workers (IFPW) was established and the Egyptian Federation of Petroleum and Chemical Workers became an affiliate. Its president, Anwar Salamah, was a director of the IFPW and later a vice-president.

The International Trade Secretariats are international organizations of unions in specific trades and industries which cooperate closely with the ICFTU. They are completely independent in their internal affairs but leave it to the ICFTU to formulate and execute general international policy and representation.[5] By virtue of its affiliation to the IFPW, therefore, Egyptian labor had an indirect contact with the ICFTU.

Egyptian labor, however, never joined the ICFTU itself. The government apparently discouraged membership because of the absence of a national confederation. When the Egyptian Confederation of Labor was finally formed in January 1957, however, it affiliated with the pan-Arab confederation instead. Shortly thereafter, the Egyptian Federation of Petroleum and Chemical Workers severed its relations with the IFPW. Similar action apparently took place relative to Egyptian membership in the ITF.[6]

The Lebanese League of Unions is a founding member of the ICFTU. But with this exception, the ICFTU has had very little success in the Arab Levant. The ICFTU, however, has made significant advances in North Africa: both the Libyan and

Tunisian labor movements became affiliates of the ICFTU in 1951, Morocco's UMT followed suit in 1955, and Algeria's UGTA joined in 1956. Aden's Trade Union Congress was also affiliated with the ICFTU in 1956.[7] Finally, Sudan's SGWTUF had its application for affiliation approved in March 1958.

Labor leaders from these organizations have held important positions in the ICFTU. Current Arab members or substitute members of its executive board are Ahmad Talili of Tunisia's UGTT, Qa'id Rashid of Algeria's UGTA, M. N. Feratian of Lebanon's League of Syndicates, and 'Abd Allah 'Ubaid of Aden's Trade Union Congress.

The ICFTU's North African membership represents a bastion of strength in the ICFTU's African and Arab programs. Significantly, the ICFTU's Fifth World Congress was held in Tunis in July 1957 in the UGTT's newly-opened "Labor Bourse." Leaders of the government, including President Bourguiba, officially took part in the welcoming ceremonies at the opening of the congress.[8] This is indicative of the esteem in which the ICFTU is held in North Africa.

THE ICFTU'S CONTRIBUTIONS IN THE ARAB WORLD

The ICFTU has provided technical aid and other services to its North African affiliates. It had won their affiliation in the first place, however, largely through its active support of the North African independence movements.

Supporting Arab Nationalism

Shortly after its founding in 1949, the ICFTU sent a delegation to North Africa to study the trade union situation. The committee, which was comprised of labor leaders from the United States, Switzerland, and France, visited Tunisia, Algeria, and Morocco.[9] The ICFTU then became increasingly involved in the North African independence movements, on the basis that the French authorities were infringing upon the trade union rights of the Arab workers. Therefore, the ICFTU sent notes to a succession of French premiers and lodged complaints against the French government in the ILO.

The struggle is still going on. The ICFTU has admitted the Algerian UGTA into membership, for example, even though its organization is proscribed by the French authorities and many of its leaders are either in jail or in exile. The ICFTU has been using funds from its International Solidarity Fund to assist interned Algerian trade unionists and their families. In 1957, the Algerian question dominated the ICFTU's entire fifth congress. When this body drafted its resolution on Algeria, therefore, the ICFTU reiterated the part of its Constitution which proclaims the right of all peoples to full national freedom and self-government.

The remarkable thing about the ICFTU's action, of course, is that the ICFTU has supported North Africa's independence from France in spite of the fact that the ICFTU itself has important trade union affiliations in France.

But the ICFTU's interest in Arab national rights has not been confined exclusively to North Africa. The ICFTU had no Egyptian affiliates, for example, but it entered the fray on Egypt's behalf during the Suez crisis. The ICFTU insisted that the United Nations be given a vital role in finding a solution to the problem. When fighting broke out, the ICFTU called for an end to it and demanded the withdrawal of the foreign troops from Egyptian territory. Thereafter, the ICFTU was concerned with both a speedy reconstruction of war damages and a thorough study of the Aswan Dam project, which had precipitated the crisis in the first place.[10]

The ICFTU, however, had an affiliate in Lebanon which justified the keen interest the ICFTU took in the civil disturbances which occurred in 1958. To be sure, the ICFTU recognized the fact that the governments of both Jordan and Lebanon had asked for British and American troops to assist them out of their respective crises. Nevertheless, the ICFTU felt that "the dispatch of troops by foreign powers, even at the invitation of governments, is not the real answer." This task, the ICFTU affirmed, belongs to the United Nations.[11]

The North African Arab trade union movements in general were associated with the ICFTU before their respective governments had attained independence. This explains why the ICFTU has enjoyed the support of the emerging governments. It also accounts for the early political bias of the movements. Nevertheless, the ICFTU undertook to direct these nascent labor movements into normal trade union channels, while supporting their nationalistic aspirations.[12]

Developing Trade Unionism

The ICFTU has provided technical and training aid in the field to its Arab affiliates. In September 1953, for example, the ICFTU sponsored a trade union training course in Tunis and repeated it in 1955. Students from Libya and Morocco also attended the session. Later in the year, the ICFTU held its Sixth International Summer School (as a seminar) at Accra. North African trade unionists were enrolled. The ICFTU's most important contribution in the field of trade union training, however, has been the establishment of a labor college in Africa. The school at Kampala began its courses in late 1958. Trade unionists from the Sudan and Aden were enrolled in its first class.

In the meantime, the International Confederation of Free Trade Unions has sponsored a number of conferences involving Arab labor unions. Its most important so far as North Africa is concerned was the African Regional Conference which was held in Accra in January 1957. This conference laid the basis for an African Regional Organization of the ICFTU. Of particular interest, a North African committee was created within this organization. The committee comprises the four North African Arab states.

The ICFTU sent a commission to the Levant in 1952 to survey labor conditions. Based on the commission's findings, the ICFTU decided to conduct trade union training programs and publish trade union literature in Arabic. An expanded program for the Levant was tentatively launched in 1955 when Nuri Budali, a former secretary general of the Tunisian UGTT, established his base in Beirut as the ICFTU's regional representative in the Middle East. He traveled extensively, visiting Egypt, the Sudan, Aden, Syria, Iraq, Jordan, and Saudi Arabia. He also began a modest program of Arab-language publications. But in November 1956 he resigned, and since then the information center in Beirut has been staffed only by a female secretary.

Except for this and the efforts of Lebanon's League of Unions, nothing else represents the ICFTU on a full-time basis in the Arab Levant. Nevertheless, various officials and groups pass through the area from time to time on behalf of the ICFTU. A direct measure of their efforts was the affiliation of the Aden TUC in 1956 and the Sudanese SGWTUF in 1958.

Providing International Worker Solidarity

The ICFTU has deplored the suppression of trade union rights in the Arab world. By various means, the ICFTU has sought to secure the freedom of association for the workers in the unorganized Arab states. Nuri Budali visited the Persian Gulf for this purpose, for example, when he was the ICFTU's representative in the Levant, but without any success. On another occasion, the ICFTU protested directly to the Secretary General of the United Nations when the workers' rights were infringed upon in the same area.[13]

The ICFTU has also backed up its affiliated organizations in their running battles with the local employers. In some areas, the ICFTU wields considerable influence. When the IPC was involved in large-scale layoffs in Tripoli in Lebanon, for example, the ICFTU was able to protest directly to the company through the British TUC. The ICFTU has also been able to help the Aden Trade Union Congress on a similar basis.

In most instances the ICFTU will send a cable of support to its affiliate in its troubles. In some cases, however, as in Aden in April 1958, the ICFTU will send a representative to the scene of the dispute. In any event, the public support of the ICFTU to a local labor organization has some bearing in resolving a dispute in its favor.

AREAS OF CONFLICT WITHIN THE ICFTU

Despite its comparative success in the Arab world, the ICFTU is faced with factors which have seriously hindered its work among Arab labor. Some of these factors are intrinsic to the ICFTU's very nature, however, and apparently cannot be changed.

Identification with Western Foreign Policy

The bulk of the membership of the International Confederation of Free Trade Unions is located in Western Europe and North America. The identification of the ICFTU with the West, therefore, is natural and a certain amount of Western bias is expected. Some of its opponents, however, have identified the ICFTU as an instrument of American foreign policy. On his visit to Africa in 1954, Vice-President Nixon went out of his way to meet the labor leaders. Since then the charges have been repeated until they are believed in some quarters that the United States is seeking to dominate Afro-Asia through its trade unions.

To be sure, the American influence upon the ICFTU is considerable. There are groups in the American labor movement, for example, who object strongly to any efforts being directed, either through the ICFTU or the agencies of the American government, toward aiding labor movements they consider offensive in the Arab world.[14] The trend is presently away from a sharp black and white distinction toward a gray area. Nevertheless, a strong feeling still persists against specific Arab countries and labor movements which are uncompromisingly anti-Israel.

The American influence in the ICFTU, of course, has also exercised the European affiliates of the ICFTU. There are two issues, however, which particularly bother the ICFTU's non-Western affiliates; viz., colonialism and Zionism.

Colonialism

Lorwin points out that Farhat Hashad of Tunisia represented the sentiments of many of the delegates at the ICFTU's Second World Congress in Milan in 1951 when he stated that colonialism was still a very real problem to the workers of Asia and Africa.[15] The second congress, therefore, adopted a resolution requesting the United Nations to conduct a thorough investigation of the problems of dependent territories.[16]

At its Fifth World Congress in 1957 in Tunis colonialism was still a big issue, particularly in regard to Algeria and Hungary. This congress reaffirmed "the free trade unions' opposition to colonialism and their determination to fight for the recognition and the application of the right of all peoples to choose their governments and of self-determination. . . ."[17]

Despite these resolutions, the ICFTU's work is hampered in Asia and Africa by fresh memories of Western colonialism. In this regard, it must be remembered that some of the ICFTU's leading affiliates are the British TUC, the French *Force Ouvrière*, and the Belgian Federation of Trade Unions. With due respect to their public stand against colonialism, they still have their own national interests to consider. The French *Force Ouvrière*, for example, did not vote for the action taken by the ICFTU in Tunisia.

Some of the European and American affiliates of the ICFTU feel that it must take a stronger position in favor of the right to self-government. The affiliates from the colonial powers, however, point to the economic implications of rapid de-colonialization. In general, they favor a process of gradualism. Ultimately, of course, this tendency is bound to be reflected to a degree in the ICFTU's official position. The ICFTU, for example, favors self-determination for the Algerians. Nevertheless, the ICFTU has also stressed the necessity of a negotiated settlement of the entire Algerian problem, involving proper consideration for French interests and citizens in Algeria. To ardent Arab nationalists, however, this is a weak position.

Zionism

Israel's labor federation, the Histadrut, had withdrawn from the WFTU in 1950 and joined the ICFTU. By virtue of geography, the Histadrut and some of the Arab labor movements fall together into the ICFTU's Middle East area (which also includes non-Arab Greece, Turkey, and Iran). Within this area the ICFTU has only two comparatively small Arab affiliates in Lebanon and Aden. The strongest affiliate in the area is the Histadrut.

On the question of Israeli membership, however, the ICFTU has no illusions regarding the detrimental effect this has upon its own relations with the Arab labor movements. Nevertheless, it has faced the issue and intends to stand by its Israeli affiliate. On the Arab-Israeli problem, the ICFTU has repeatedly stated that it can only be settled on the basis of Arab recognition of the state of Israel and on an equitable and sound solution to the problem of the Arab refugees.

As for the Israelis, they also have no illusions regarding their awkward position vis-à-vis the Arab states in the ICFTU. The Israeli delegates were publicly reminded of the "toleration" extended them in Tunisia, an Arab state, at the ICFTU's fifth congress. On its part, however, the Histadrut sought to demonstrate at this same congress its attempts to get along with Arab workers. It brought along an Arab "Israeli" trade unionist as an official delegate to the congress. Nevertheless, the Lebanese delegate probably summed up the sentiments of the ICFTU's Arab membership when he publicly urged the congress to exclude Israel from the ICFTU.[18]

Aside from any moral issues, one must keep several relevant factors in mind to understand the ICFTU's stand on Israel. On the one hand, it is only fair to say that considerable pressure has been brought to bear upon the ICFTU in favor of both Israel's membership and its cause. As a matter of fact, these same pressure groups sometimes tend to hang the ICFTU's entire Middle East program on Arab recognition of Israel. On the other hand, it must also be remembered that the Histadrut itself is a large force in the ICFTU. In fact, compared with any organized Arab labor movement in the Middle East area, as defined by the ICFTU, the Histadrut is huge.[19] Finally, there is some doubt that the Arab states to whom Israeli affiliation is particularly objectionable would join the ICFTU even if Israel were excluded. To date, none of its Arab affiliates have left the ICFTU because of Israel's affiliation.[20]

On the basis of these factors there is little likelihood that the ICFTU will change its attitude toward Israeli affiliation. In the meantime, however, the stand of the ICFTU will continue to exercise its Arab affiliates.

POSITIVE NEUTRALITY

It would have been simple for the pan-Arab labor movement to establish itself as a regional organization affiliated as a bloc to either the WFTU or the ICFTU.[21] Either of these would probably have offered both technical and financial aid. The International Confederation of Arab Trade Unions, however, immediately let it be known that it would remain an independent movement and would not follow either camp.[22]

This was in line with the strong current of neutrality that was developing in the Afro-Asian world regarding the struggle between the West and the Communists. Egypt had taken the most outspoken stand among the Arab states, of course, when it officially adopted a position of positive neutrality. This is also the basic principle in the Egyptian-sponsored ICATU's international relations.

A Neutral Arab Labor Movement

Essentially this policy allows the pan-Arab movement to cooperate with other international labor groups, but not to join them. Nevertheless, the Arab confederation has repeatedly stated that it is not opposed to its affiliates being also allied to either the WFTU or the ICFTU, so long as their interests did not conflict with the principles and aims of Arab nationalism and the

ICATU's Constitution.[23] Indeed, the ICATU shares the affiliation of the Libyan LGWU with the ICFTU and the Sudanese SWTUF with the WFTU. The ICATU itself has joined neither.

To be sure, the following is taken out of context. Nevertheless, it handily summarizes the meaning of positive neutrality in the field of labor. The following is taken from a letter from the secretary general of the ICATU to his counterpart in the ICFTU:

> Trade unionists and workers in any part of the world have prime responsibility to bring about international understanding and peace. They feel linked to each other. Their actions do not aim only at raising their standards of living and conditions of work but also to fight any system which deprives individuals from freedoms whether political, economic or social. You pursue in the ICFTU a definite line to this effect, you wage a fight against dictatorships, concentration camps, and forced labor, you support democracy, freedom of nations etc. These are fine principles and all workers of the world can only agree with them. Likewise the principles contained in the Constitution of the WFTU are ideals for the working class the world over, and have at once found support from all workers of the world. If the world trade union movement is divided today it is not on differences of aims but on how to achieve the goals. The chasm between East and West today does not serve any purpose. We are called upon to choose, but our choice was to consolidate our newly won victories, independence and national emancipation so as to fit ourselves for our role and international mission. We will not be dragged into political conflicts which are foreign to ours; our hands are still full with those of emancipation. . . .[24]

The pan-Arab movement itself, however, has participated in the activities of both the ICFTU and the WFTU. Indirectly, for example, the ICATU participated in the ICFTU-sponsored African Regional Conference held in Accra in January 1957.[25] But in particular, the pan-Arab movement has attended a number of WFTU meetings. A delegation including the secretary general of the ICATU, for example, took part in the WFTU's Fourth World Congress in Leipzig in 1957.

Anti-ICFTU Orientation

A series of factors brought the new movement into a conflict of interests with the ICFTU. The pan-Arab movement, for example, identified the ICFTU with the West, Imperialism, and Zionism. Moreover, a conflict between the two movements was almost unavoidable by virtue of the ICFTU's dominant position in parts of the Arab world.

The pan-Arab movement, therefore, took on an obvious anti-ICFTU bias. In the same ICFTU-ICATU correspondence mentioned above, the Arab confederation's secretary general went on to provide the basis for this feeling:

We can only judge our friends by their acts. We are ready to forget past acts although they are very near to our memories. We have suffered only from one kind of imperialism, the dominance of the West. . . . These are memories of the past. If, however, we take the very recent events we find that the West seems to preserve our dark memory of them. The war in Algeria, the attack on Egypt, the coercive settlement of the Zionists in Palestine, the aggression on Aden, Goa, Indonesia, and the aggressions against the people of the Far East are further examples. On top of all this the West tries to impose on us pacts attaching the Afro-Asian people to their carriage. We want to be left to manage our own affairs. We need no tutelage, direction or paternalistic so-called 'aid'. If you are our brothers help us to oust the Western Powers from our lands, factories and economies, and declare that you are against such degrading and naive paroles as "Vacuum" in this or that region. . . . We are quite awake and detest such inferences as . . . "they are only exchanging one domination for another." We have bitterly fought, and still are, for our liberties; the taste of liberty is too sweet to be exchanged for any other diet.

OPEN CONFLICT BETWEEN THE ICATU AND THE ICFTU

During the first year of its founding, the ICATU and the ICFTU worked in uneasy truce in their common area. In general, the ICFTU tended to ignore the new movement as being of no moment in the Arab world. A public break between the two, however, came in July 1957 on the second day of the ICFTU's congress in Tunis.

Apparently without any forewarning, the ICFTU's secretary general launched into an attack from the floor of the conference against the International Confederation of Arab Trade Unions. He concentrated on three things: the Arab confederation had done nothing so far to improve the conditions of workers; it is nothing but a political instrument; and it is anti-Israel. He concluded by saying that "if this Arab Confederation does not exist for the purpose of demanding that social conditions be improved then it has no right to exist." [26]

The reactions of the congress were mixed. Some felt that the attack had been ill-advised and could destroy any good will there might have been in the uncommitted Arab Levant toward the ICFTU's cause. The North Africans in particular took this position.[27] There were others, however, who supported the secretary general's position, including the Lebanese delegation.[28]

The attack provoked a strong reaction on the part of the

Arab confederation. Indeed, there was no doubt as to the feelings of either party prior to this point. Nevertheless, the pan-Arab movement has been careful to point out that its open attacks against the ICFTU began only after it had opened the attack at Tunis.

Thereupon an open attack against the ICFTU erupted in the Arab press. The secretary general of the Egyptian Confederation of Labor co-authored a pamphlet on the evils of the ICFTU in Africa and Asia.[29] Open letters were exchanged between the two parties. In addition, the attack without a doubt precipitated the withdrawal of the Egyptian Federation of Petroleum and Chemical Workers from the IFPW.

The attack on the pan-Arab movement, however, had one distinct virtue: it clarified the issue between the ICFTU and the International Confederation of Arab Trade Unions.

POSITIVE NEUTRALITY AND THE WFTU

The Communist-dominated WFTU, of course, found the existing situation ideally suited to its own purposes. The fact that the WFTU had almost nothing to lose in the area led to its immediate strong support of the new movement. In fact, merely by alienating Arab labor from the ICFTU, the WFTU had considerable to gain.

The position of virtual monopoly enjoyed by the ICFTU in North Africa alone provided a common ground for cooperation between the ICATU and the WFTU. Therefore, to the extent the ICATU was prejudiced against the ICFTU, the Arab movement became predisposed towards the Communist-dominated WFTU.[30]

The recent events in Iraq have shown, however, that imperialism is not a Western monopoly. The second congress of the ICATU in April 1959, therefore, roundly condemned international Communism and resolved that Communists should be eliminated from the ranks of Arab labor.

Nevertheless, the overt activities of the Communists in Iraq's labor movement have not driven the International Confederation of Arab Trade Unions into the arms of the anti-Communist ICFTU. On the contrary, these events have merely given full body to the pan-Arab labor movement's stand of positive neutrality and non-alignment — with either the West or the Communists.

VII

COMMUNISM AND THE PAN-ARAB LABOR MOVEMENT

Communism enjoyed a spell of unwonted freedom in the Arab world until late 1958. For the most part this freedom came about because Communism had identified itself as the friend of Arab nationalism and the foe of imperialism. "Imperialism" of course connoted only the West. For as the ICATU's secretary general stated, the Arabs' experience of Russian imperialism was indeed negligible — up to that time.[1]

COMMUNISM'S IDENTIFICATION WITH ARAB NATIONALISM

Until recently, Communism's appeal had been largely to the intelligentsia. Many of the Communist leaders, for example, came from well-to-do families. Laqueur has pointed out, therefore, that it was not unusual that thirty-nine Baghdad lawyers volunteered to defend four Communist leaders (three of them lawyers themselves) in Baghdad in 1947.[2] Similarly, two hundred Damascus and Beirut lawyers volunteered to defend the Lebanese Communist, Mustafa 'Aris, at his trial in 1949. Then in 1951, fifty-seven Lebanese lawyers offered to defend Jordan's Communist leader, Fuad Nasir, at his trial.

By identifying itself with resurgent Arab nationalism, however, Communism had been able to broaden its base and reach the Arab masses, the workers and the peasants.

Appeal to the Masses

It has only been within the past few years that an effective appeal could be directed to the workers and peasants. The feudalistic pattern prevailing in industry and on the land had previously precluded such an approach. Recent developments in industrialization and the more recent land reforms, however, which were accompanied by legislation favorable to associations of industrial and farm workers, have broadened the scope a popular appeal may take.[3]

It should be noted, however, that the Communist leaders among the Arabs had been long and well prepared for the new offensive. Fuad Nasir, for example, had been closely connected with the nascent Palestinian and Jordanian labor movements.[4] Mustafa 'Aris was the head of the Lebanese Communist labor federation, in addition to being head of the local Communist Party. At the founding conference of the WFTU in 1945 in Paris, he had been elected a member of the executive committee for the Middle East.[5]

But it was the Syrian Communist leader, Khalid Bakdash, who actually set the pattern for the new approach. He did this in the report which he delivered before the plenary session of the Central Command of the Communist Party in Syria and Lebanon which was held in January 1951:

> Our job during the present stage is to muster the broad masses and especially the workers and peasants. . . . We must establish broad foundations and bases among the workers and fellahin for the Peace movement and for all mass movements and organizations. . . . Our work in the union field must be on a mass basis and in depth. To date it has been confined mainly to the better-paid elements and the rest have been almost entirely neglected. . . . . Work among the fellahin requires clarity in the Party's position *vis-à-vis* the various groups of which the rural population is composed. At present, however, this clarity is not easy to attain since we have little experience in working in the rural areas and have little knowledge of the subject. . . .[6]

Combatting "Colonialism"

In the meantime, by virtue of the Communist espousal of Arab nationalist causes, a strong rapport developed between Arab labor and the Communist-controlled World Federation of Trade Unions. Under the pretext of aiding "colonial" labor movements, the WFTU seized upon the opportunities offered by the prevailing crises in the Near East.[7] Until recent events in Iraq dissuaded them, some Arab circles apparently labored under the impression that the WFTU's cooperation sprang only from the deep wells of worker solidarity.

To be sure, on a number of issues the positions of the ICFTU and the WFTU were very similar. Nevertheless, the WFTU's support was often more spontaneous than the ICFTU's on a given issue and, in general, more acceptable because of the latter's identification with the West. It is only fair to state, however, that while the WFTU's stand was always identical to the Soviet foreign policy, the ICFTU's position was occasionally at variance with the national foreign policy of some of its most powerful affiliates.

On the armed conflict over the Suez Canal, for example, the ICFTU's stand was diametrically opposed to the policy of the governments of three of its powerful affiliates: the British TUC, the French *Force Ouvrière*, and the Israeli Histadrut. On the troop landings in Lebanon and Jordan, the ICFTU was also opposed to the policy of the government of its influential American affiliate, the AFL-CIO.

COMMUNIST PENETRATION OF ARAB LABOR MOVEMENTS

Communists have been able to penetrate various Arab labor movements. In some instances, the penetration has been in such depth that it has led to affiliation with the Communist-led WFTU. In other cases, it has enabled the Communists to control the movements completely. In all instances, however, the Communist influence has been far out of proportion to the number of activists.

Affiliated Movements

In Algeria the trade union structure followed the French pattern, each metropolitan center being represented by local branches. By virtue of these beginnings, Algerian workers were of necessity affiliated with the Communist-dominated CGT. Under nationalist pressure, however, two autonomous centers sprang up in Algeria. The smaller of the two, with about 5000 members, became the *Union Générale des Syndicats Algériens*. It is affiliated with the WFTU. The UGSA, however, is proscribed like the other nationalist organizations and its normal trade union activities, therefore, have ceased.

Lebanon's Communist Federation of Labor Unions is also illegal, but still continues to operate.[8] This federation, located in Beirut, has been closely associated with the WFTU since its founding. Because of its strategic position in the Levant, Beirut has been used as a base for the WFTU's Arab propaganda. The printers' union of the WFTU's Lebanese affiliate, for example, apparently plays a vital role in this activity. The federation's most important affiliate, the Hotel, Restaurant, and Coffee House Workers' Union, it has been suggested, also is strategically important because it serves large numbers of foreigners passing through Beirut to other parts of the Near East.[9]

Associated Movements

The Sudan Workers' Trade Union Federation (SWTUF) had been considered one of the WFTU's most stalwart supporters in the Arab world. Although it apparently had not been formally affiliated to the WFTU, the SWTUF had actively supported the WFTU's program and just as vigorously opposed the ICFTU. The labor department's annual report described the SWTUF's leaders in 1953 as "self-avowed Communists." [10] Like the Lebanese Communist federation, the SWTUF had refused to register with the government.

Communist leadership had plagued the SWTUF for years and brought about a covert affiliation with the Communist-dominated World Federation of Trade Unions. At its world congress in 1957, the SWTUF's secretary general al-Shafi' Ahmad al-Shaykh was elected to a WFTU vice-presidency. In the meantime, however, the Sudan government has cracked down upon Red trade union activities. Al-Shafi' Ahmad al-Shaykh and several other leaders of the SWTUF have been sentenced to prison terms.

The lack of WFTU affiliates, however, does not represent a lack of Communist strength in the Arab labor movements. On the contrary, there is evidence of a strong Fifth Column which rises to the need on call. In this connection, Lichtblau has indicated that the WFTU has adopted the general strategy of having its affiliates merge where necessary with larger nationalist movements and lose their identity, in the hope of capturing the movement from within.[11] He mentions the former Tunisian and Moroccan WFTU affiliates in this regard.

The WFTU had also claimed affiliates in Egypt and Syria. In fact, one of the leaders of a so-called "Syrian Labor Congress" was a member of the WFTU's executive committee. In 1957, however, the WFTU agreed that henceforth it would cooperate only through "official" Syrian trade union organizations.[12] Apparently this congress, therefore, has disassociated itself from the WFTU and has merged in the Syrian government-approved labor movement.

Captured Movement

Trade union activities had been suspended initially under the new regime in Iraq. In the meantime, however, "constituent" committees were created in anticipation of the government's approval. It has been indicated that seventy-four of these committees had existed at the end of 1958 and had elected a general council.[13] Therefore, when government approval was granted in January 1959, the trade union movement was off to a running start. Moreover, the framework for a general confederation was already established.

The consensus is that the Communists have captured for the moment the largest part of the labor movement in Iraq. Most evidence points this way. Not necessarily corroborative, but indicative is the message which the WFTU indicated it had received in February 1959 from an Iraqi trade union confederation: "Loyal to the principles of international working class solidarity, we send our most cordial greetings to the WFTU. . . ." [14]

In February 1959, this Iraqi movement organized its first mass meeting in Baghdad. It was claimed that forty thousand workers and peasants participated in the meeting under banners bearing the slogan: "Workers of Iraq Unite." Later on in Iraq's first celebration of May Day in 1959, again thousands of workers and peasants paraded through Baghdad carrying banners proclaiming: "Long Live the Alliance of Workers and Peasants — The Foundation of Social Progress," and "Workers of the World Unite." [15] The first day of May every year has been declared "Labor Day." [16]

To be sure, not all Iraqi labor is controlled by the Communists. The International Confederation of Arab Trade Unions, for example, claims it received the affiliation of an Iraqi confederation of labor comprising thirty central labor unions. Apparently, however, this pro-ICATU organization's activities have been severely curtailed through pressures generated by the Communist-controlled organization, which sent the following message to the Cairo-based ICATU in February 1959: *

*Author's note: In the meantime, the Iraqi federation has affiliated with the WFTU. The trend, however, currently appears to be moving against the Communists in the Iraqi labor movement.

We urge our brothers in the ICATU, sending them our warmest greetings on their anti-imperialist struggle, to defend trade union rights in the Arab countries and to take a firm stand against any violation of these rights, such as is taking place in the UAR and the Sudan.[17]

Fraternal Relations

Finally, the WFTU has maintained fraternal relations with workers in a number of other Arab states, some of which have no organized labor movements. Table 10 is indicative of the general sweep of the WFTU's activities in the Arab world.[18]

Table 10. Arab Representatives at the Fourth World Congress of the World Federation of Trade Unions in 1957

Country	Delegates or Observers
Algeria	1
Egypt	2
Iraq	2
Jordan	1
Kuwait	2
Lebanon	6
Saudi Arabia	1
Sudan	8
Syria	25

At this same congress, the Sudanese SWTUF won a seat on the WFTU's executive bureau. In addition, Algerian, Lebanese, and Sudanese affiliates were elected to the WFTU's executive committee, to which Syria was also entitled one deputy member. And finally, Algerian and Lebanese trade unionists won seats on the WFTU's general council. In the meantime, the WFTU has also been directing its appeal to the growing number of Arab female workers. Syrian and Lebanese delegates, for example, attended the WFTU-sponsored First World Conference of Women Workers which was held between 14–17 June 1956 in Budapest.

COOPERATIVE PROGRAMS

On the basis of the rapport which had been established between the World Federation of Trade Unions and the pan-Arab movement, the two organizations embarked upon joint programs of mutual interest.

An Afro-Asian Labor Federation

As part of its Constitution, the International Confederation of Arab Trade Unions has pledged itself to take steps to establish an Afro-Asian federation of labor.[19] This aim is shared with the WFTU, albeit with somewhat different purposes in mind.

The WFTU, for example, has been attempting to establish an Afro-Asian neutral labor federation since 1953. If successful, of course, this would either neutralize the present ICFTU affiliates or even alienate them completely from their parent organization. To be absolutely sure of this, however, the "neutral" federation is to be dominated by the powerful Communist labor movements of China and Russia itself.

Table 11. Membership in the ICFTU and WFTU in Non-Communist Asia and Africa in 1957

	WFTU	ICFTU
Africa	77,457	1,651,864
Asia and Australasia	1,884,400	7,009,288

Source: Accurate membership figures for the WFTU in Asia and Africa are difficult to come by, for since 1951 the WFTU has not published a breakdown of its membership by individual countries. The figures here presented have been extrapolated from the U.S. Department of Labor *Directories*, referred to in Table 9, and are for December 1957. The figures represent only the non-Communist areas and, therefore, exclude the WFTU's membership in Red China — 13,700,000, North Korea — 467,000, Mongolia — 27,500, and North Viet Nam — 300,000 members. Somewhat lower estimates of both the WFTU's and the ICFTU's membership are given by George R. Donahue, *The World Federation of Trade Unions: Facts About a Communist Front* (New York, n.d.), and in the ICFTU, *Report of the Fifth World Congress* (whose membership figures, however, are for the beginning of 1957).

The importance of doing something about the ICFTU in Africa and Asia is apparent in the comparative figures given in Table 11. In addition, it should be noted that almost 80 per cent of Africa's total trade union membership falls within North Africa, where the ICFTU is dominant almost to the exclusion of the other two movements.[20] In fact, this represents the strongest factor binding the WFTU and the ICATU together in their common Afro-Asian interest.[21]

To be sure, Afro-Asian cooperation itself had begun earlier on a formal basis at Bandung. Nevertheless, the Afro-Asian movement took on new proportions in Cairo which has sponsored a series of Afro-Asian conferences. The spectrum of Afro-Asian cooperation now includes, for example, the establishment of an Afro-Asian trade union federation. Trade unions, therefore, took part in the Afro-Asian Solidarity Conference which was held in Cairo in December 1957.

In the meantime, however, considerable groundwork had been done prior to this conference to get it to endorse an Afro-Asian labor federation. The ICATU, for example, had canvassed a number of Afro-Asian labor organizations; they issued joint communiqués on their community of interests in the proposed federation.[22] The conference itself issued the following resolution:

> With a view to mobilizing the broad sections of peoples of the Asian and African countries for combatting imperialism, promoting world peace, attaining and maintaining national independence, developing national economy and improving living conditions of the people, the Conference deems it necessary to promote unceasingly solidarity and cooperation in trade unions and cooperative movements of Asian and African countries, within the spirit of the Bandung Conference. Taking into consideration the wishes and aspirations of the workers and many trade unions and cooperative movements of Asia and Africa for solidarity and cooperation, the Conference urges that when appropriate circumstances mature a trade union conference of the Afro-Asian countries as well as a cooperative conference be convened with broad representation to discuss their common problems.[23]

Afro-Asian cooperation, of course, is well within President 'Abd al-Nasir's Three-Ring concept, which comprises Arabs, Africans, and the vast Muslim population stretching from the Atlantic to the Philippines. His concept embraces neutrality, but in the positive sense of molding these neutral forces into a positive "Third Force" between the West and the Communists. Afro-Asian labor represents only one of the areas in which this new force apparently is intended to be wielded in international affairs.

The Afro-Asian movement, however, has also been ideally suited to the purposes of the Communists.[24] They have, therefore, sought to capture and use the movement as a front organization. There were indeed a few weak objections raised against Russian participation in the Afro-Asian movement.[25] Nevertheless, at the first conference in Cairo Russia won a strategic position on the permanent secretariat of the Afro-Asian Solidarity Council, and has continued to play an important role in the Afro-Asian movement.

The projected Afro-Asian labor federation, however, has run into considerable opposition in the meantime from various quarters. In particular, the ICFTU has opposed the proposed organization by launching its own large-scale regional programs in Africa and Asia. In consequence, an Afro-Asian labor federation has not yet been established.

In Support of Algeria

A more successful example of cooperation between the two organizations was the International Trade Union Conference for Solidarity with the Workers and People of Algeria which was held in Cairo between 12–15 September 1958. Eighteen international labor organizations participated.

The official organs of both the ICATU and the WFTU indicate that the decision to hold this conference had been reached at the WFTU's Fourth World Congress in Leipzig in 1957. Further preparatory discussions were then held at a meeting of the executive council in Prague in July 1958, which representatives of the ICATU attended.[26]

To be sure, the conference generated international support for Algeria, particularly among the North African organizations which attended. Nevertheless, the implications of WFTU cosponsorship sharply restricted the conference's appeal. In fact, except for the Arab organizations, the conference appealed in the main only to WFTU affiliates.

COMMUNIST ATTEMPTS TO DOMINATE THE ICATU

While the ICFTU apparently was determined to meet the challenge of the new International Confederation of Arab Trade Unions head on, the WFTU obviously had decided instead to cooperate with it wherever possible.

Cooperation

In fact, it appears that the WFTU's Arab affiliates were under orders to show a positive attitude toward the establishment of the International Confederation of Arab Trade Unions and to cooperate or merge with it wherever possible.[27] Therefore, although their affiliation was rejected, Lebanese affiliates of the WFTU sought to participate in the founding conference of the ICATU in 1956. The Communist-dominated Sudanese SWTUF, however, was accepted as an affiliate in May 1957.

In any attempt to explain the relationship between the pan-Arab labor movement and the WFTU, an allowance must be made for the gestures of worker solidarity the WFTU had shown. Regardless of its motives, the WFTU had indeed supported the various Arab nationalist causes. The ICATU, therefore, responded in turn by cooperating in various WFTU-sponsored activities. In particular, many exchange visits were arranged. Representatives of the ICATU and its affiliates took part in innumerable activities held in the USSR and its satellites.

Under the new regime, Communists in Egypt have been suffered from time to time but have never been in favor. Laqueur has pointed out, for example, that after the revolution in 1952 most of the Communists in prison were released and came to the support of the military junta.[28] When the government crushed a Communist-led strike a few months later, however, the Communists turned against the Free Officers, leading to strong mutual opposition which lasted until 1955/56.

Then Egypt began to occupy itself with a broad-scale anti-Western foreign policy, and again the government released a number of Communists from prison. While some of these were prevented from returning to active politics, many of the intellectuals returned to positions exercising considerable influence upon the Liberation Rally, its successor, the National Union Party, and the labor movement.

In view of these circumstances, therefore, it is not at all strange that quite often both the propaganda and actions of the pan-Arab labor movements were hardly distinguishable from those of the WFTU.[29] The influence and direct involvement of the WFTU in Arab labor affairs, however, became more obvious with each successive Near Eastern crisis. The high point was reached in the middle of 1958. At this point, in fact, it looked as if the International Confederation of Arab Trade Unions had become an affiliate of the WFTU.

Immediately following the Iraqi revolution and the American and British troop landings in July 1958, the WFTU called an extraordinary session of its executive committee to be convened in Prague.[30] The sole item on the agenda was: "Events in the Middle East, and Action by the Working People in Defense of Peace." Of particular interest, however, was the presence of "fraternal guests" from Egypt, Syria, Iraq, the Sudan, and the International Confederation of Arab Trade Unions. It was recorded that during this special session "new bonds of unity were forged between the World Federation of Trade Unions and the International Arab Trade Union Confederation. . . ."[31]

Contention

In the meantime, however, there were those in Cairo who were seriously concerned over the strong influence the WFTU was gaining over the pan-Arab labor movement. In fact, some felt that the ICATU was in serious danger of losing what was supposed to be one of its distinctive characteristics, non-alignment.[32]

The recent Communist alarums in the Arab world, however, have finally reversed the tide: Communism and Communists are now in disrepute among pan-Arabists. Relationships between the pan-Arab labor movement and the WFTU, therefore, are not at all what they used to be. While exchange visits are still carried on, for example, they are under stricter controls than before. Moreover, the ICATU reaffirmed at its second congress its support of positive neutrality and non-alignment with either the West or the Communists.

There is no question at all, of course, that the pan-Arab labor movement and the Communist-dominated WFTU were closely aligned. Nevertheless, to interpret this as an attempt of the WFTU to "use" the International Confederation of Arab Trade Unions is only half correct; the reverse is just as true.

VIII

PROBLEMS AND PROSPECTS OF THE PAN-ARAB LABOR MOVEMENT

In view of the pan-Arab labor movement's past history and current events, what are the movement's prospects for the future? There are no definitive answers, of course, but there are certain broad conclusions one can reach.

MOUTHPIECE OF ARAB LABOR

It is the stated aim of the International Confederation of Arab Trade Unions to become the mouthpiece of Arab labor. To be sure, the movement has not yet come close to achieving this goal. In fact, the pan-Arab labor movement has succeeded as a labor movement only in the UAR. The movement's success elsewhere is in direct proportion to the conformance of the ideas of Arab nationalism existing there with those prevailing in the United Arab Republic.

A number of experts in the field have come to the conclusion that the ICATU is not really a *pan-Arab* labor movement. Instead it is a captive movement with an essentially political purpose. The Assistant U.S. Secretary of Labor for International Affairs, for example, recently stated:

> Mr. Nasser was quick to appreciate the political significance of labor in his attempt to achieve power in the Arab world. When the existing union leadership in various Arab countries proved reluctant to cooperate with him, he organized the International Confederation of Arab Trade Unions as an instrument for reaching directly from Cairo to the workers of the other countries.[1]

This factor perhaps more than any other has kept the ICATU from becoming in fact the mouthpiece of Arab labor. Nevertheless, this feature has not discouraged the participation of all the legitimate Arab labor leaders. Some have joined and supported the new movement with the hope that they might turn it into a legitimate trade union force for the improvement of the position of Arab labor. In this regard, they feel that a legitimate pan-Arab labor organization is quite as logical as the International Federation of Christian Trade Unions (IFCTU).

To date, the International Confederation of Arab Trade Unions has been essentially a political movement and has been involved in every Egyptian-sponsored international action. ICATU-sponsored calls for political action, however, have not gone unanswered in the Arab world; Arab labor has responded. To be sure, the response has varied. But when Arab labor failed to respond *pro forma*, it was often due to controls imposed by the national governments which appear to have been more discriminating than the working classes. In any case, however, it should be pointed out that the responses of labor were most often merely reflexes of Arab nationalism rather than signs of true Arab working class solidarity.

The normally accepted functions of trade unionism have been relegated in the ICATU to a secondary position behind political goals, allegedly out of expediency. For liberation from foreign interference in Arab affairs and feudalism has been set as the primary goal. If one agrees with this point of view, of course, it would be unfair to state that the ICATU has no real interest in bona fide trade unionism. It is merely a matter of timing.

And in this regard, perhaps Egyptian sponsorship may not be at all undesirable. For as Professor Harbison recently stated:

> Egypt has had a successful social and political revolution; its ruling regime is honest and comparatively stable; and it has a sense of direction. The Revolution broke the grip of the landed aristocracy on political and economic life. To be sure, the Nasser regime rules the country by force, yet it appears to command the enthusiastic support of practically all elements of the population. Although Nasser's ambitions in foreign affairs are not designed to please the West, the fact remains that he is committed to internal economic improvement, industrial development, and a greater measure of social welfare and education for the people.[2]

In summary, the Arab labor confederation will without a doubt continue to be actively engaged in many "abnormal" union activities, under Egyptian sponsorship. To be sure, the movement will also attempt to rid itself of the political stigma. Nevertheless, since the pan-Arab labor movement feels that workers' rights cannot be won without momentous political changes in the Arab world, the best one can hope for is a better balance between political and legitimate trade union activities.

RELATIONS WITH THE COMMUNISTS AND THE WEST

In the international field, the Arab labor confederation has often attempted to run with the fox and hunt with the hounds. At least, so it has appeared to impartial observers. This inconsistent stand has then been rationalized on the basis of positive neutrality.

The Arabs, however, are in dead earnest when they speak of positive neutrality. And neutrality itself, of course, is not at all an unreasonable reaction of the newly-freed states to the conflict between their old colonial masters in the West and the new force of the USSR.

One eminent Arab historian, for example, points out that the newly-independent Arab states recognize their continued dependence upon the outside world for arms, capital, technical assistance, higher education, and markets. Nevertheless, they cherish their recently-won independence above all else.[3]

But unfortunately, non-involvement in the conflict between the West and Communism connotes to many Afro-Asians a guarantee of freedom from both responsibility and involvement in the outcome of the struggle between the two forces. This stand prevails despite the fact that its pitfalls become increasingly more patent in the Afro-Asian world.

The very fact that the International Confederation of Arab Trade Unions follows a course of positive neutrality immediately made it suspect in the eyes of the anti-Communist International Confederation of Free Trade Unions. By the same token, however, the Communist World Federation of Trade Unions welcomed the new movement into the Arab world in the hope that the ICATU would join the WFTU in its struggle against the ICFTU in the area.

The two organizations have worked very closely together, for two reasons. In the first place, the ICFTU has been the dominant international labor organization in the Arab world. It has been particularly strong in North Africa which both the ICATU and the WFTU hope to penetrate. Then in the second place, the ICATU has identified the ICFTU with Western imperialism and Zionism. The ICATU, therefore, has cooperated in a number of ways with the WFTU. The principle involved appears to have been that the enemy of my enemy is my friend rather than a common Communist philosophy.

To be sure, however, individual Arab Communists and fellow travelers have also played an important role in the affairs of the International Confederation of Arab Trade Unions. Their influence has been far out of proportion to the number of activists. In consequence, the ICATU was brought into close cooperation with the WFTU on joint programs which were often merely fronts for the Communists. Nevertheless, the ICATU apparently was not a completely blind follower; it in turn was trying to use the WFTU to enhance its own position among the Arabs.

Events in Iraq seem finally to have opened the eyes of the ICATU to the danger inherent in cooperation with the WFTU. The former close rapport, therefore, no longer exists between the two organizations. Nevertheless, these events have not driven the ICATU into the arms of the anti-Communist ICFTU as some might hope. On the contrary, the ICATU now appears to be wary of alignment with both the Communists and the West.

EXPANSION IN THE ARAB WORLD

Founding members of the International Confederation of Arab Trade Unions were from five Arab states: Egypt, Jordan, Lebanon, Libya, and Syria. After three years the movement has added only one other affiliate, the Sudanese SWTUF. Another affiliate is claimed in Iraq, but its existence is dubious.*

The International Confederation of Arab Trade Unions has gained considerable ground in the United Arab Republic by virtue of the state-sponsored consolidation of the trade union movement. In the Lebanon, however, there is little likelihood of the ICATU winning the affiliation of the remaining two legal federations or of having the same degree of influence it had prior to the Lebanese disturbances of 1958.

No appreciable change is expected in the relations between the Libyan LGWU and the ICATU. It must be remembered, however, that the allegiance of the LGWU is torn between the ICATU and the ICFTU, which are at odds with each other.

In the meantime, the ICATU has lost ground in the two remaining states represented in its founding membership. These are Jordan and Sudan. In the first, the government has in effect cut off relationships between organized labor in Jordan and the

* Author's note: Apparently Aden has now also affiliated with the ICATU.

ICATU. In the other, the Sudanese government has jailed the leadership of the SWTUF and has banned all trade union activities. The immediate prospects of renewing the former close relationships, therefore, are very poor.

Persian Gulf States

Trade unionism is still unknown in this area, except in Iraq. And there the Communists apparently control organized labor to the undoing of all attempts by the ICATU to gain entree. Except in Iraq and Bahrain, trade unions are still illegal in the other Arab states of the Persian Gulf.

In Bahrain itself there is little prospect of labor joining the ICATU in the foreseeable future. In the first place, affiliations with international labor organizations are presently frowned upon. In the second place, while labor federations are not specifically mentioned in Bahrain's recent labor legislation, by the same token they are not a priori permitted. In fact, the argument of silence in this instance leads one to the contrary view: the entire portion dealing with federations in the draft law had been deleted by the Ruler.

Labor in Kuwait, Qatar, and Saudi Arabia remains unorganized. Kuwait is the nearest to legalizing trade unions, having a draft law providing freedom of association for labor. Saudi Arabia, on the other hand, has a Royal Decree in effect which absolutely forbids labor associations.

It can probably be safely stated that, with the exception of Iraq, the sympathies of Arab labor in the Persian Gulf area are generally pro-ICATU. Moreover, if labor had the organization and the opportunity it would probably join the International Confederation of Arab Trade Unions.

The governments in the area, however, are on the whole reluctant to allow labor participation in ICATU-sponsored activities. This is not so much that they are anti-labor or anti-ICATU as they are frightened of Communist leadership which has so often showed its hand in connection with labor in the area.

The Maghreb

Without any question, the largest and best organized Arab labor movements are located in North Africa. In addition to a community of general North African interests, these labor organizations have several things in common regarding labor: e.g., membership in the ICFTU; a desire to establish their own North African Federation of Labor within the framework of the ICFTU; an active interest in the pan-African program of the ICFTU; and a growing interest in a pan-Arab labor program.

Relative to the last, it seems to be the consensus among the North African labor organizations that the ICATU is a misguided movement. Yet, in general they have all been very careful to refrain from openly criticizing the ICATU. As for their individual relations to the ICATU, however, they are not at all uniform.

For example, the Libyan LGWU joined the ICATU as a founding member but has also retained an active membership in the ICFTU. The Moroccan UMT has not affiliated with the ICATU, but does maintain fraternal relations with it. The Tunisian UGTT, however, in general refuses to have anything to do with the International Confederation of Arab Trade Unions.

For the present, therefore, prospects for further expansion in North Africa seem poor for the International Confederation of Arab Trade Unions.

CONCLUSION

On the basis of present indications, the International Confederation of Arab Trade Unions in its present form will probably not succeed in becoming the mouthpiece of all Arab labor. Nevertheless, to say this is not to say that the ICATU has been a failure. On the contrary, like a catalytic agent the ICATU has greatly accelerated the development of labor consciousness in the backward areas of the Arab world.

More importantly, however, the International Confederation of Arab Trade Unions reflects the growing importance of Arab labor in the Arab world. The ICATU is probably the first step in the direction of an all-embracing Arab labor organization. We can look for more developments in this important area.

NOTES

CHAPTER 1

THE SETTING FOR A PAN-ARAB LABOR MOVEMENT

1. Cairo daily newspaper, *al-Ahram*, no. 2533, 14 April 1956.

2. 'Abd al-'Alim al-Mahdi, *This is the International Confederation of Arab Trade Unions* (in Arabic; Cairo, 1958), p. 9.

3. International Confederation of Arab Trade Unions (ICATU), *The Constitution* (Cairo: El Tanani Press, 1957), Article 7, B. An almost psychopathic fear of Communism infiltrating the labor movement has been one of the chief factors behind the governments' reactionary attitude.

4. J. A. Hallsworth, "Freedom of Association and Industrial Relations in the Countries of the Near and Middle East," *International Labour Review*, 70.5:364 f. (November 1954).

5. Clark Kerr *et al.*, "The Labour Problem in Economic Development, a Framework for a Reappraisal," *International Labour Review*, 71.3:3-15 (March 1955).

6. Doreen Warriner, *Land Reform and Development in the Middle East*, Royal Institute of International Affairs (London, 1957), *passim.*

7. As Khalid Bakdash admitted in his report before the plenary session of the Central Command of the Communist Party in Syria and Lebanon, held in January 1951: *For the Successful Struggle for Peace, National Independence, and Democracy We must Resolutely Turn toward the Workers and the Peasants* (abridged translation by Harold W. Glidden, *Middle East Journal*, 7.2:206–221 [Spring 1953]).

8. Doreen Warriner, *Land and Poverty in the Middle East*, Royal Institute of International Affairs (London, 1948), p. 38. Agricultural laborers in Egypt, for example, were not included in the provisions of the labor law passed in 1942 to legalize trade unions because, according to the rapporteur who introduced the law, their inclusion would open the door to Communism.

9. International Labour Organization (ILO), Petroleum Committee, Fifth Session, Caracas, 1955, Report III, *Human Relations in the Petroleum Industry*, Third Item on the Agenda, Report prepared by the ILO (Geneva, 1955), p. 71.

10. Frederick Harbison and Ibrahim Abdelkader Ibrahim, *Human Resources for Egyptian Enterprise* (New York, 1958), pp. 189 f.; G. L. Harris, *Egypt* (New Haven: Human Relations Area Files, 1957), pp. 186 ff.

11. ILO, "Report of the Committee on Freedom of Employers' and Workers' Organizations," *Official Bulletin*, 39.9:588 (1956).

12. *Ibid.*

13. United Nations, *Social Conditions in the Middle East*, Preliminary Report on the World Social Situation (New York, 1952), p. 159A.

14. United Nations, *Review of Economic Conditions in the Middle East* (New York, 1952), p. 29.

15. Kerr *et al.*, *op. cit.*

16. R. S. Porter, *Report on the Census of Employment in Bahrain, 1956* (Beirut, 1957); Government of Iraq, Ministry of Economics, Principal Bureau of Statistics, *Report on the Census of Services and Service Industries in Iraq for 1957* (Baghdad: Government Press, 1958); Republic of Lebanon, Ministry of National Economy, *Industrial Census, 1955* (Beirut, 1957).

17. For example, the average number of persons employed in "manufacturing" shops in Bahrain is only 2.5 persons. Porter, *op. cit.*, pp. 6 f.

18. T. B. Stauffer, "Labor Unions in the Arab States," *Middle East Journal*, 6.1:83–88 (Winter 1952).

19. W. B. Fisher, *The Middle East, a Physical, Social and Regional Geography* (London, 1950), pp. 209–212.

20. For example, Bahrain's service industry while of comparatively modern origin is now one of its largest industries. Porter, *op. cit.*, pp. 5, 24 ff.

21. The ILO was founded under the League of Nations and is now one of the specialized agencies of the United Nations. The following Arab states are members: Iraq, Jordan, Lebanon, Libya, Morocco, Sudan, Tunisia, and the United Arab Republic. Saudi Arabia and the Yemen are members of the United Nations but do not belong to the ILO. Saudi Arabia, however, subscribes to the ILO publications.

22. G. E. Lichtblau, "The Politics of Trade Union Leadership in Southern Asia," *World Politics*, 7.1:84–101 (October 1954).

23. *Ibid.*

24. In Aden, Bahrain, and Sudan, to mention only a few.

25. The ICFTU and the WFTU represent, respectively, the non-Communist and the Communist international labor blocs.

26. International Labour Conference, *Provisional Record*, No. 32, 42nd Session, 31st Sitting (Geneva, 1958), pp. 485–488.

27. "Oil and Social Change in the Middle East," *The Economist* (2 July 1955), p. 14.

28. Royal Decree No. 17/2/23/2639, 11 June 1956, published in the official gazette, *Umm al-Qura*, No. 1621, 22 June 1956, and broadcast by *Radio Mecca* on the same day.

29. ICFTU, *Report of the Fifth World Congress: Held in Tunis 5–13 July 1957* (Brussels, 1958), p. 104.

30. ICATU, *Constitution*, *op. cit.*

31. *Al-Ahram*, No. 2533, 14 April 1956.

32. Al-Mahdi, *op. cit.*, p. 9.

33. David H. Finnie, *Desert Enterprise: The Middle East Oil Industry in its Local Environment* (Cambridge, Massachusetts, 1958), *passim.*

34. *Wataniyyah* from *watan,* "a country."

35. *Qawmiyyah* from *qawm,* "a people."

36. "On Reading Arab Omens," *The Economist* (5 October 1957), pp. 19, 20.

37. Al-Mahdi, *op. cit.,* p. 27.

38. "The labor movement is always a reaction and protest against capitalism." Taken from J. R. Commons, "Labor Movement," *Encyclopedia of the Social Sciences,* VIII (London and New York, 1930–35), 682.

39. *Studies in Labor and Industrialization.* This is a four-university research project on the labor problem in economic development: University of California (Berkeley), University of Chicago, Harvard University, and Massachusetts Institute of Technology. Publications have appeared in various journals between 1954 and the present and have been reprinted for private circulation.

Chapter II

THE INTERNATIONAL CONFEDERATION OF ARAB TRADE UNIONS

1. Zaki Badaoui, *Les Problèmes du Travail et les Organizations Ouvrières en Égypte* (Alexandrie: Société de Publications Égyptiennes, 1948), pp. 20, 21.

2. This has been particularly true in North Africa. Nevertheless, see N. A. Faris and M. T. Husayn, *The Crescent in Crisis, an Interpretative Study of the Modern World* (Lawrence, Kansas, 1955), p. 51, regarding labor's role in the nationalistic struggles for independence elsewhere in the Arab world.

3. *Al-Ahram,* 3 December 1955.

4. Cairo daily, *al-Jumhuriyah,* 20 March 1956.

5. M. al-Biqa'i, "*L'Évolution du Mouvement Ouvrier en Syrie depuis le Régime Ottoman jusqu'à l'Indépendence,*" (Damascus: Bureau des Documentations Syriennes et Arabes, 1957). (Mimeographed.)

6. *Al-Jumhuriyah,* 4 April 1956.

7. *Ibid.;* ICATU, *Constitution, op. cit.,* Article 4.

8. This organization was set up by the government to take the place of a confederation, on an unofficial basis. It was replaced by the Egyptian Confederation of Labor, which was established in January 1957.

9. ICATU, *Constitution, op. cit.,* Articles 18–26.

10. The ICATU had scheduled the second congress for 24 March, the anniversary date of its founding, which has since been designated "Labor

Day." The congress was postponed a month, however, because Ramadhan fell in March that year.

11. *Al-Jumhuriyah*, 4 April 1956. At this time all of the founding members were without all-inclusive national confederations. In fact, confederations did not even exist in either Egypt or Lebanon.

12. ICATU, *Constitution, op. cit.*, Articles 27 ff.

13. The list of officers was taken from a release issued by the ICATU, 6 May 1959. The functions and duties of the officers, however, have been largely drawn from the Constitution. The second congress may have amended the sections of the Constitution dealing with the functions of the officers. At the time of writing, however, this information was not available.

14. ICATU, *Constitution, op. cit.*, Article 34.

15. The Arab League was established as a regional organization in March 1945. Its founding members are: Egypt, Iraq, Jordan, Lebanon, Saudi Arabia, Syria, and Yemen. Libya joined the League in March 1953 and the Sudan in January 1956. In February 1958 Egypt and Syria merged into one state: the United Arab Republic. Tunisia and Morocco joined in October 1958. In addition, the provisional government of Algeria, the Palestinian government in the Gaza Strip, and the Shaikhdoms of Kuwait and Bahrain are often represented at its meetings.

16. See John Price, "Industrial Committees of the ILO," *International Labour Review*, 65.1 (January 1952), for a general picture of the role and purposes of the committees.

17. E.g., vocational training and technical education, wages, recruitment, labor-management machinery, contract labor, employee services, housing, etc. See ILO, *Official Bulletin*, vols. XXX ff. (1947 ff.), *passim*; and ILO, Petroleum Committee, *Reports*, *passim*. In particular, its report on contract labor in the petroleum industry has had an important impact on Arab labor in the petroleum industry.

18. Cairo daily, *al-Qahirah*, 29 May 1954. It was considering recommendations regarding training, education, and savings plans for petroleum workers.

19. *Al-Ahram*, 2 December 1955.

20. The Arab League, General Secretariat, Department of Social Affairs, *Report of the Committee on Labor Legislation in the Arab States* (in Arabic; Cairo, 1956).

21. Anwar G. Chejne, "Egyptian Attitudes toward Pan-Arabism," *Middle East Journal*, 11.3:253–258 (Summer 1957). He indicates that although pan-Arabism had existed in Egypt, it did not have a broad appeal until the present regime came into power.

22. *Al-Ahram*, 14 April 1956. ICATU's newly elected secretary general was asked to carry its thanks personally to President Gamal 'Abd al-Nasir and Major Tu'aimah, head of the labor section; the latter for his "tremendous efforts" in support of the new movement.

23. ICATU, *Constitution, op. cit.*, Article 3. Headquarters can be re-

located by a decision of the congress. The first congress was convened in Damascus, and the second in Cairo. Its meetings are to be held by rotation in all the countries represented in the federation (Article 19).

24. *Ibid.*, Articles 13–17. ICATU's fees and dues would not support its broad activities. Therefore, it allows "donations which do not run counter to the aims of the Federation." Acceptance of such donations is to be approved by the executive council.

25. *ILO Press Release*, ILO 14 A, 26 May 1958.

26. E.g., the Organization of American States, the European Coal and Steel Community, and the Council of Europe.

27. UNESCO Paper, E/3082, 14 March 1958. The Arab League is designated by the ILO as an "Inter-Government Organization" in this agreement.

28. International Labour Conference, *Record of Proceedings*, 40th Session, 1957 (Geneva, 1958), p. 588. Three international labor organizations enjoy consultative status in the International Labour Organization: the ICFTU, the WFTU, and the International Federation of Christian Trade Unions (IFCTU).

29. Al-Mahdi, *op.cit.*, p. 44. "The Arab governments recognized the Confederation the moment the ILO recognized its existence."

30. Harris, *op. cit.*, p. 186.

31. Chejne, *loc. cit.*; Charles Issawi, "Negotiation from Strength? A Reappraisal of Western-Arab Relations," *International Affairs*, 35.1:1–9 (January 1959). The latter points out that while opinions differ as to what form that unity should take, "there is widespread acceptance of Egypt's leadership."

Chapter III

THE PHILOSOPHY OF THE INTERNATIONAL CONFEDERATION OF ARAB TRADE UNIONS

1. ICATU, *Constitution, op. cit.* The aims of the new federation were reduced from an original thirty-five in the draft constitution to sixteen in the approved constitution.

2. See *al-'Ummal al-'Arab* (in Arabic) official organ of the ICATU, published in Cairo, *passim.* (The first issue appeared in November 1957.)

3. The text of the draft constitution appeared on 3 March 1956 in the Beirut weekly *al-Waqt*, which describes itself as "the organ of Arab labor unions." A summary also appeared in *al-Ahram*, 9 March 1956, but under the title "Arab Democratic Federation of Labor."

4. The approved text is available either in English, ICATU, *Constitution, op. cit.*, or in Arabic, both of which can be obtained from the ICATU

headquarters in Cairo. The complete Arabic text is also found in the Egyptian Ministry of Social Affairs and Labor, Directorate General of Labor, *Census of Labor Unions and Federations in the Republic of Egypt, December 1956* (in Arabic; Cairo: Government Press, n.d.), pp. 143–152.

5. Charles Issawi, "The United Arab Republic," *Current History*, 36.210: 65–69 (February 1959).

6. These were Egypt, Jordan, Lebanon, Libya, and Syria.

7. See Table 1, Chapter II.

8. Only two of the four "legal" Lebanese federations had affiliated themselves with ICATU.

9. ICATU, *Constitution, op. cit.*, Article 7, B.

10. See ICATU secretary general's statement to the press in *al-Ahram*, 14 April 1956, and its president's statement in the Jerusalem daily, *Falastin*, 26 May 1956.

11. The "conventions" represent the International Labour Organization's recommendations which member states are urged to embody in their own laws. In the January 1958 issue of its official organ, the ICATU ranks the Arab states in the ILO according to the number of conventions each has ratified. Morocco ranked highest, then Egypt and Tunisia, Syria and Iraq, etc. (ICATU, *al-'Ummal al-'Arab*, no. 2 (January 1958) pp. 18, 19).

12. Government of Bahrain, *The Bahrain Employed Persons Compensation Ordinance, 1957* (Bahrain, November 1957); *The Bahrain Labour Ordinance, 1957* (Bahrain, November 1957); Government of Iraq, Ministry of Social Affairs, Directorate-General of Labour and Social Security, *Labour Law (No. 1 for 1958)* (Baghdad, 1958).

13. It is commonly agreed that the labor member of Bahrain's tripartite labor law advisory committee was coached by outsiders during the drafting of Bahrain's labor law. (See Government of Bahrain, *Annual Report for Year 1956* [Bahrain, 1957], p. 5; H. W. Hazard, *Subcontractor's Monograph on Eastern Arabia* [unpublished; New Haven: Human Relations Area Files, no. 51, 1956], 190; and W. A. Beling, "Recent Developments in Labor Relations in Bahrayn," *Middle East Journal*, 13.2:156–169. [Spring 1959].)

14. Iraq's draft labor law was scrapped after it had been completed, because it did not conform to ILO conventions. Without a doubt, the Arab League's emphasis upon the importance of these conventions in Arab labor legislation had a bearing on this action. At any rate, an ILO expert was brought in to bring the proposed legislation into line with the ILO conventions. (International Labour Conference, *Record of Proceedings*, 40th Session, *op. cit.*, pp. 99 f.

15. ILO *Legislative Series 1936* (Iraq 2).

16. Government of Iraq, *Labour Law (No. 1), op. cit.*, Article 113 (1).

17. Government of Kuwait, "The Kuwait Draft Labor Law: The Civil Section," *Annual Report of the Department of Social Affairs, 1957* (in Arabic; Kuwait, 1957), pp. 55–72.

18. See Salah Ayyub, "Industrial Relations," *al-Mujtama'* (in Arabic; published monthly by the Department of Social Affairs, Kuwait), 1.6:4 ff. (September 1958); and 'Abd al-Mughni Sa'id Salamah, "Collective Bargaining," *al-Mujtama'*, 1.8:6 ff. (November 1958).

19. Muhammad Tawalbek, "Jordan Workers resist Eisenhower Doctrine," *World Trade Union Movement*, no. 12 (December 1957), pp. 33 f.

20. ICATU, *Constitution, op. cit.*, Article 6.

21. As broadcast over *Radio Cairo* and *Radio Voice of the Arabs*, 18 April 1959.

22. Many other labor organizations, however, have also supported the Algerian independence movement, viz., the ICFTU and the WFTU.

23. See Beirut dailies *al-Diyar*, 19 June 1958, and *al-'Amal*, 26 May 1958. The ICATU was criticized, however, by its Lebanese affiliate for interfering in a domestic issue.

24. ICATU, *al-'Ummal al-'Arab*, no. 1 (November 1957), pp. 21–23. This is often referred to as its most important meeting.

25. The WFTU's official organ, *World Trade Union Movement* (London, 1956 and 1957), *passim.*

26. Republic of Sudan, Ministry of Social Affairs, *Annual Report 1956/57* (Khartoum, 1957), p. 41. Following the invasion of Egypt, the SWTUF refused to cooperate in any way with French or British civil airlines passing through the Sudan. Thereupon, the employers suspended some of the striking employees and this precipitated the calling of a four-day strike. Following subsequent demonstrations and general disorder, the government then declared a state of emergency.

27. See Cairo dailies *al-Jumhuriyah* and *al-Qahirah*, 2, 3 November 1957; Beirut dailies *al-Diyar* and *al-Sharq*, 4 November 1957; ICATU, *al-'Ummal al-'Arab, passim*; and al-Mahdi, *op. cit., passim.*

28. *Voice of the Arabs* (Cairo), 6 December 1956. An announcement was broadcast that the ICATU had drawn up plans for resisting any measures imperialism might take in the future; *ibid.*, 18 October 1957. It was reported that the ICATU had sent a cable to President Eisenhower threatening to stop the flow of oil and to close the Suez Canal if there should be any aggression against Syria.

29. ICATU, *Constitution, op. cit.*, Article 6.

30. Damascus daily, *al-Jamahir*, 27 April 1959. Delegates from Aden, Algeria, Iraq, and Saudi Arabia presented testimony regarding social and labor conditions in their countries. Apparently, Nasir Sa'id from Saudi Arabia offered pictorial evidence. In actual fact, however, he does not represent the workers of Saudi Arabia except by his own appointment. He fled the kingdom a few years ago after getting into a scrape and has been living in exile since.

31. Al-Mahdi, *op. cit.*, p. 39.

32. Muhammad Jawad al-'Abbusi, *Oil in the Arab States,* A Series of Lectures delivered to the Students of the Department of Economics and

Social Studies, 1955 (Cairo: The League of Arab States, Institute of Advanced Arab Studies, 1956; translated from Arabic into English by the Research Translation Office, Beirut, 1958), p. 108.

33. Frederick H. Harbison, "Two Centers of Arab Power," *Foreign Affairs*, 37.4:672–683 (July, 1959). He points out that Egypt dramatically demonstrated that she can operate the Suez Canal despite the departure of foreign management. Moreover, Egypt possesses and operates, almost exclusively with Egyptian personnel, some of the most modern textile factories in the world. In addition, there are fertilizer plants, cigarette factories, railways, an airline, iron and steel works, and other modern industrial undertakings — all managed and operated by Egyptians. Finally, Egypt is the only nation among the so-called underdeveloped states which has operated its own petroleum production and refining, without expatriate top management (following sequestration of British interests in Egypt).

Chapter IV

CONSOLIDATION OF THE PAN-ARAB LABOR MOVEMENT

1. Partly based on Abdel Raouf Abou Alam, *The Labor Movement in Egypt* (Washington, 1955); M. T. Audsley, "Labour and Social Affairs in Egypt," *Middle Eastern Affairs, Number One*, St. Antony's Papers, No. 4 (London, 1958), pp. 95–106; William J. Handley, "The Labor Movement in Egypt," *Middle East Journal*, 3.3:277–292 (July 1949); Harbison and Ibrahim, *op. cit.*; and U. S. Department of Labor, Bureau of Labor Statistics, *Summary of the Labor Situation in Egypt*, International Cooperation Administration, Office of Labor Affairs (July 1955).

2. Law No. 85/1942, *Official Gazette*, No. 171 (in Arabic; Cairo: Government Press, 6 September 1942); ILO *Legislative Series*, 1942 (Egypt 1).

3. *Official Gazette*, No. 157 *bis*, 8 December 1952 (in Arabic); ILO *Legislative Series*, 1952 (Egypt 3).

4. Hallsworth, *op. cit.*, 70.5:368–384 (November 1954) and 70.6:526–541 (December 1954).

5. Cairo daily *al-Jumhuriyah*, 22 November 1958.

6. E.g., the first president of the Egyptian Confederation of Labor and the present secretary general of the International Confederation of Arab Trade Unions came from the Petroleum and Chemical Workers' Federation.

7. *Saut al-'Ummal*, 1.1 (in Arabic; Cairo, 25 February 1957). In October 1952, Colonel 'Abd al-Nasir asked labor to commit itself to the cause of the revolution. From these beginnings, Major 'Abd Allah Tu'aimah emerged as the Revolutionary Command Council's labor boss. Thereupon, the labor section which he directs organized trade union training courses to instruct

labor leaders on the operation of trade unions within the framework of Egyptian legislation.

8. Decree Law No. 8, *Official Gazette*, *op. cit.*, no. 5, 13 April 1958; *al-Ahram*, 2 May 1958; a circular by Anwar Sadat, secretary general of the National Union, entitled "Organizing the Labor Movement Under the Auspices of the National Union," which appeared in *Akhbar al-'Ummal*, 8 May 1958 (in Arabic).

9. Anwar Salamah also resigned from the presidency of the Egyptian Chemical and Petroleum Workers' Federation, an affiliate of the ICFTU-affiliated International Federation of Petroleum Workers, and from the presidency of the Shell Oil Company Oil Workers' Union to which he has since returned.

10. Harbison and Ibrahim, *op. cit.*, pp. 177 f.

11. Yusif A. Sayigh, "Management-Labour Relations in Selected Arab Countries: Major Aspects and Determinants," *International Labour Review*, 77.6:519–537 (June 1958).

12. See Frederick H. Harbison and Ibrahim A. Ibrahim, "Some Labor Problems of Industrialization in Egypt," *The Annals of the American Academy of Political and Social Science*, 305:114–124 (May 1956), for a discussion of the situation. Apparently the strike leaders at Kafir al-Duwar were Communists.

13. Legislative Decree No. 317 of 8 December 1952, *Official Gazette*, *op. cit.*, No. 157 *bis*, 8 December 1952 (in Arabic); ILO *Legislative Series*, 1952 (Egypt 1); Republic of Egypt, Ministry of Commerce and Industry, *Opportunities for Industrial Developments in Egypt*, Report to U.S. Government Foreign Operations Administration Under Contract SCC-21504 C-58780, Arthur D. Little, Inc., Cambridge, Mass., 20 December 1954 (Cairo: Government Press, 1955), pp. 157–162. It is interesting to note the recurrence in this report of the following phrase: "Employers *seem to* have the right to discharge . . . ." (Italics are the present author's.) But in actual practice, by virtue of the *quid pro quo* arrangement with labor (no strikes: no dismissals), employers rarely had this right.

14. See *Report of Husain al-Shafi'i, Minister of Social Affairs and Labor, Presented in the First Portion of the First Legislative Session of Parliament* (in Arabic; Cairo: Government Press, August 1957); and Jean G. Économidès, "L'Action du Nouveau Régime Égyptien dans les Domaines Économique et Social," *L'Égypte Contemporaine*, no. 286, pp. 5–44 (October 1956). They review labor legislation promulgated under the new regime and other government efforts in support of labor.

15. "The Egyptian Union Movement," *The Egyptian Economic and Political Review*, 3.8:15 ff. (April 1957). Labor was intended to "play a positive role in the coming parliament to improve labour legislation and raise the moral and material standards of the Egyptian worker."

16. WFTU, *World Trade Union Movement*, *op. cit.*, No. 8, pp. 13 f. (August 1957), carried a statement by the president of the Egyptian Con-

federation of Labor to this effect. (The aims and philosophy of the ICATU are discussed in the preceding chapter.)

17. Very little of recent origin has been written on the Syrian labor movement. The most recent brief treatments are the following: 'A. 'Aziz Allouni, "The Labor Movement in Syria," *Middle East Journal*, 13.1:64–76 (Winter 1959); Hallsworth, *op. cit.*; the sections by Charles Issawi in *Syria*, 2 vols., ed. by Raphael Patai (New Haven: Human Relations Area Files, 1956); and Stauffer, *loc. cit.*

18. ILO *Legislative Series*, 1946 (Syria 1).

19. Republic of Syria, *Statistical Abstract of Syria, 1955*, Ministry of National Economy, Directorate of Statistics (Damascus: Government Press, 1956). At the end of 1954, 10,870 workers were organized in industry; 5091 in commerce; 2867 in construction; 4531 in transportation; 375 in mining; 1972 in public utilities; 2140 in service industries; and 2403 in government services. (N.B., statistics from different official and quasi-official sources are sometimes in conflict with each other; therefore, the total membership here is not identical to that for 1954 in Table 4.)

20. Thomas B. Stauffer, "The Industrial Worker," in *Social Forces in the Middle East*, ed. Sidney N. Fisher (Ithaca, 1955), pp. 83–98.

21. Source: Republic of Syria, Ministry of Labor and Social Affairs, Trade Union Section, *Schedule of Employer and Employee Labor Unions Registered in Syria until the End of 1957* (in Arabic: Damascus, n.d.), pp. 33 f.

22. *Le Progrès Égyptien* (Cairo), 23 April 1959. By this date the trade unions are expected to have reorganized themselves to be able to effect a merger.

23. In 1954, a splinter group broke away from the regional Federation of Trade Unions in Damascus and established the Progressive Federation of Trade Unions. A similar group established the Progressive Federation of Trade Unions in Homs in 1957. Until recently both were independent federations. In September 1958, however, Tal'at Taghlabi of the Progressive Federation in Damascus became president of the confederation. Steps were then immediately taken to merge in one district federation the two federations which previously had been competing with each other in both the Homs and Damascus districts. Nevertheless, it should be noted that although all existing federations are affiliated to the confederation, not all of the unions are affiliated to federations. As of August 1958, there were 202 unions affiliated with the Confederation of Trade Unions in Syria. (Cf. Beirut daily *al-Hayat*, 10 August 1958, which carried an announcement of the confederation to this effect.)

24. Under Secretary of State Murphy, *Labor's Concern with Foreign Affairs*, U.S. Department of State Bulletin, January 17, 1957, pp. 84–86. He cites an incident in connection with the trade fair held in Damascus in 1954, which indicates the extent of the Communists' efforts to capture Syrian labor: "To build the Russian pavilion, 1200 [Syrian] workers were

hired. They were paid 10 pounds for an 8-hour day in contrast to the normal 2–3 pounds which workers on other pavilions received. Overtime was generous and medical care good. . . . Some of these workmen said to themselves: 'If this is the way they treat you in Russia, I'm for them.'"

25. E.g., Syria was reported to have had more delegates at the WFTU's Fourth World Congress in Leipzig in 1957 than the combined representatives of the other eight Arab states attending the conference. (*Texts and Decisions of the Fourth World Trade Union Congress, Leipzig, 4–15 October 1957*, published by the WFTU [London, n.d.].)

26. U.S. Department of Labor, Bureau of Labor Statistics, *Labor Developments Abroad* (April 1958), p. 9.

27. Hallsworth, *op. cit.*, No. 5, pp. 364 f.

28. International Bank for Reconstruction and Development, *The Economic Development of Jordan* (Baltimore, 1957), *passim*; L. T. Schweng, *Report of the Hashemite Kingdom of Jordan Agricultural Development* (Amman, 1952), *passim*; and Jerusalem daily *Falastin*, 23 May 1958.

29. See *The Report of Brother Zaidan Yunus, Secretary General of the Federation of Trade Unions in Jordan, on the Labor Movement in Jordan from its Founding to the End of September 1955* (mimeo. in Arabic; Amman, n.d.). Very little has been published in English on the Jordanian labor movement. This report and the following book are the best summaries of the movement up to 1956: 'Ali 'Anad Kharis and Salah 'Abd al-Karim al-Safadi, *The Trade Union Movement in Jordan* (in Arabic; Amman, n.d.).

30. Law No. 35, *Official Gazette of the Hashemite Kingdom of Jordan* (in Arabic; Amman, 16 February 1953), No. 1134.

31. *Report of Brother Zaki al-Shaykh Yasin, Secretary General of the Federation of Trade Unions in Jordan, on the Labor Movement in Jordan from September 1955 to the End of March 1958* (mimeo. in Arabic; Amman, n.d.).

32. *Ibid.* This government-approved statement was issued by Zaki al-Shaykh Yasin who replaced Zaidan Yunus in the federation. It was labor's reply to reports that the government had outlawed trade unions.

33. Republic of Lebanon, Ministry of National Economy, *Industrial Census — 1955*, I and II, prepared with technical technical assistance of Economic Research Institute, American University of Beirut (Beirut, 1957–58). The census excluded establishments: (1) with less than five employees; (2) concerned entirely with repair work; (3) engaged entirely in final assembly of products; and (4) presenting certain difficulties, viz., olive oil extraction industry and certain public service industries.

34. Based in part on U.S. Department of Labor, Bureau of Labor Statistic, *Summary of the Labor Situation in Lebanon*, International Cooperation Administration, Office of Labor Affairs (July 1956); and Edward W. Samuell, Jr., "A Contribution to the Study of Lebanese Labor Syndicates" (unpublished M.A. thesis, American University of Beirut, 1952).

35. ILO *Legislative Series*, 1946 (Lebanon 1). The labor code does not apply to wage-earners of the government and municipal services. Therefore, they are not entitled to organize in trade unions. The exclusion also applies to agricultural labor, except in connection with commerce or industry.

36. Based on the author's personal correspondence with Lebanese labor leaders.

37. E.g., the second congress of the ICATU was opened by reading from the Koran. (Cf. *Le Progrès Égyptien*, Cairo, 25 April 1959.)

38. E.g., the League of Unions' representative at the ICFTU's congress in Tunis in 1957 defined the ICATU as a "political Confederation."

39. See Beirut dailies *al-Zaman*, 29 May 1958, and *al-Tallighraf*, 30 May 1958.

40. Beirut daily *al-'Amal*, 26 May 1958. Similar restraint concerning internal affairs occurred in the fall of 1956 just prior to elections: the Lebanese affiliates objected to the opening of an ICATU regional office in Tripoli.

41. The daily *Bairut al-Masa*, 25 November 1958.

42. See Beirut daily *al-Hayat*, 30 August 1958, and *al-Ahram*, 6 September 1958.

43. E.g., both the League of Unions and the Federation of Unions of Workers and Employees in North Lebanon have retained their memberships in the ICFTU and the ICATU, respectively. The latter's secretary general was recently re-elected assistant secretary general in the ICATU.

44. Benjamin Higgins, "Entrepreneurship in Libya," *Middle East Journal*, 11.3:319–323 (Summer 1957).

45. United Kingdom of Libya, Central Statistics Office, Ministry of National Economy, *Census of Employment and Production in Urban Areas, Part I, Registration of Premises in which Persons were Gainfully Occupied during 1956* (n.d.).

46. The following is based in part on U.S. Department of Labor, Bureau of Labor Statistics, *Summary of the Labor Situation in Libya*, ICA, Office of Labor Affairs (June 1958).

47. Law No. 6 of 1951, *The Tripolitania Gazette*, No. 4, 1 May 1951, p. 47; Law No. 25 of 1951, *The Cyrenaica Gazette*, No. 30, 1 February 1952, p. 23. In March 1958, however, the provincial laws were replaced by a federal law which is applicable to the entire kingdom. (Cf. Labor Act No. 100 of 1957, *The Official Gazette of the United Kingdom of Libya*, No. 4, 17 March 1958; and ILO Legislative Series, 1957 [Libya 2].)

48. The Republic of the Sudan, Ministry for Social Affairs, Population Census Office, *First Population Census of the Sudan 1955/56: 21 Facts about the Census*, prepared by Karol Józef Krótki (Salzburg, 1958); Saad Ed Din Fawzi, "Labour Force of Sudan," in *The Population of Sudan: Report on the Sixth Annual Conference*, Philosophical Society of Sudan,

Reports given at the University of Khartoum in January 1958 (Salzburg, 1958).

49. The following is based in part on Saad Ed Din Fawzi, *The Labour Movement in the Sudan 1946–55* (London, 1957), and the *Annual Reports* of the Sudanese Ministry of Social Affairs.

50. *Sudan Almanac 1958: An Official Handbook*, compiled in the information Office of the Republic of the Sudan (Khartoum, 1958), pp. 132–141. Ten of these unions, however, were employers' unions.

51. Helen Kitchen, "Trade Unions: Communist Stronghold," *Africa Special Report*, 4.1:12 ff. (January 1959).

52. The Republic of the Sudan, Ministry for Social Affairs, *Annual Report 1955/56* (Khartoum, n.d.); *ibid., Annual Report 1956/57*. These reports indicate the strong sympathies of the Department of Labor with the anti-Communist group.

53. *Ibid.* In June 1957, the SWTUF's president attended the International Labour Conference in Geneva as a representative of the ICATU.

Chapter V

THE MISSION OF THE PAN-ARAB LABOR MOVEMENT IN THE ARAB WORLD

1. Issawi, *Current History, loc. cit.*

2. At its second congress in April 1959, the ICATU announced the affiliation of an Iraqi movement. This will be discussed later in the chapter.

3. Cf. U.S. Department of Labor, Bureau of Labor Statistics, *Summary of the Labor Situation in Tunisia*, ICA, Office of Labor Affairs (March 1958); and *Subcontractor's Monograph on Tunisia* (unpublished; Human Relations Area Files, No. 63: New Haven, 1956), pp. 249 ff.

4. U.S. Department of Labor, Office of International Labor Affairs, *Directory of Labor Organizations, Directory of Africa* (Washington, 1958). Recently, foreign unions were prohibited from operating in Tunisia (Law 59–4 of 10 January 1959). This affected a few French unions which had persisted in Tunisia after Tunisian independence had been won from France. Citizens of other countries, however, may become members of Tunisian trade unions. (U.S. Department of Labor, Bureau of Labor Statistics, *Labor Developments Abroad* [April 1959], p. 22.)

5. Tahir al-Hadad, *The Tunisian Workers and the Appearance of the Trade Union Movement* (in Arabic: Tunis, 1346 A.H. [1927–28 A.D.]). A Tunisian labor leader, Muhammad 'Ali, established a purely Tunisian movement apart from the CGT in 1923. It was suppressed shortly there-

after and he was exiled. The UGTT considers this movement as its legitimate ancestor.

6. ICATU, *al-'Ummal al-'Arab*, no. 1 (November 1957), p. 22. Apparently the ICATU invited al-Habib 'Ashur, head of the rival UTT, to visit ICATU headquarters in Cairo. It seems that the AFL-CIO (through its European representative) was also interested in the UTT, but for different reasons. ("Labor's Role Abroad," *The New Republic*, 11 March 1957, pp. 6, 7.)

7. Anon., "Géopolitique de la Tunisie Syndicaliste," *Revue Politique et Parlementaire* (Paris), 224.679:504–510 (June 1958).

8. ICFTU, *Report on the Fifth World Congress*, *op. cit.*, pp. 313 ff. This was the reply of the UGTT's secretary general to an attack which had been made against the ICATU on the floor of the ICFTU's fifth congress in Tunis.

9. This was no empty gesture on the part of the UGTT. One of its former secretaries general, Nuri Budali, served as the ICFTU's first Middle East representative based in Beirut. He was called back to Tunis in 1956.

10. See U.S. Department of Labor, Bureau of Labor Statistics, *Summary of the Labor Situation in Morocco*, ICA, Office of Labor Affairs (June 1959); ICFTU, *The ICFTU and the Workers of Morocco* (Brussels, 1956); Jean and Simonne Lacouture, *Le Maroc à l'Épreuve* (Paris, 1958); and *Subcontractor's Monograph on Morocco* (unpublished; Human Relations Area Files, No. 62: New Haven, 1956), pp. 301 ff., for accounts of the history and development of the movement.

11. Source: U.S. Department of Labor, Office of International Labor Affairs, *Directory of Labor Organizations, Africa*, *op. cit.* But the membership listed by the ICFTU in 1957 was 300,000 members. Similarly Tunisia's UGTT was carried at 150,000 members instead of 225,000 (ICFTU, *Report of the Fifth World Congress*, *loc. cit.*).

12. See ICFTU, *Report of the Fifth World Congress*, *op. cit.*, pp. 399 ff., for the complete text of the speech of al-Mahjub ibn al-Sadiq: "The Moroccan Federation of Labour did not think it advisable to participate in the Accra Conference. It might be as well to give the reasons for this. In the first place, the UMT did not take part in the preparation of this Conference, to which we attach exceptional importance. Nor did we, despite our requests, receive any documents which were to serve as a basis for the discussion in this Conference. This is why it was impossible for us to attend it, without being mandated by and without having consulted our governing bodies . . . ."

13. *Ibid.*

14. ICATU, *al-'Ummal al-'Arab*, *op. cit.*, no. 2 (January 1958), p. 6.

15. *Ibid.*, no. 3 (May 1958), p. 22.

16. *Ibid.*, no. 5 (October 1958), p. 10.

17. *Ibid.*, p. 11.

18. Source: *Directory of Labor Organizations, Africa*, *op. cit.* The appli-

cation of the USTA for affiliation in the ICFTU was rejected in 1957, "after an enquiry had shown that the USTA was not representative of workers in Algeria." A similar organization, sponsored by the rival FLN/UGTA for Algerian labor in France, *L'Amicale Générale des Travailleurs Algériens* (AGTA), was established on 13 May 1957. Apparently it was dissolved in 1958 as an "illegal" organization. In addition, of course, a number of purely French unions exist in Algeria.

19. Thomas Hodgkin, "The Battle for the Maghreb," *The Political Quarterly*, 29.4:348–355 (October-December 1958).

20. *Union Générale des Travailleurs Algériens*, "Pour la Libération Nationale et un Syndicalisme Libre," *Bulletin*, no. 2, pamphlet published in Tunis (n.d.), which gives a synopsis of the early meetings.

21. *Press Release*, *PP/L/sh-Com. 15/58*, issued by the Geneva office of the ICFTU on March 10, 1958, following a conference of representatives from the North African trade union centers which had been held in Geneva under the auspices of the ICFTU: "During the conference, the leaders of the four national centers announced that considerable progress had been made with a view to uniting the four existing North African organizations into one. They welcomed the ICFTU decision to set up a regional organization for the whole of Africa, to which the united *Maghreb* center would be affiliated."

22. ICATU, *al-'Ummal al-'Arab*, No. 5 (October 1958), p. 3, provides a list of the countries, organizations, and delegates.

23. *Ibid.* The names of the Tunisian organization and delegation are not given. Libya was not represented.

24. The American bases in Morocco represent a sore point, over which the UMT in particular had been exercised (cf. Moroccan newspaper *al-Istiqlal*, 18 October 1958: "The existence of the American bases is incompatible with the policy of Moroccan independence"). This sentiment, of course, found a strong response in the pan-Arab labor movement. The second congress of the ICATU, therefore, resolved: "Arab workers cheer their friends in Morocco for their struggle for full independence and complete expulsion of occupying armies. The Arabs are confident that the people, cooperating with a popular Government in Morocco, will be able to sweep away the occupying forces and realize complete independence."

25. David Finnie, "Recruitment and Training of Labor: The Middle East Oil Industry," *Middle East Journal*, 12.2:127–143 (Spring 1958). Including Iran, the oil producing companies in the area employ something over 100,000 persons.

26. Another Egyptian delegate and two Lebanese delegates attended the founding conference.

27. *Proceedings, Second World Congress of the International Federation of Petroleum Workers, at Rome, Italy, June 24–28, 1957* (Denver, n.d.). Two delegates from the Association of IPC Employees and Workers in

the Lebanese Republic attended, as well as an observer from the Labor Syndicate of Mobil Oil in Lebanon.

28. Al-Mahdi, *op. cit.*, p. 44, characterized the IFPW as an instrument of Western imperialism. Israel's membership in the IFPW was also one of the reasons given for the withdrawal.

29. *Akhbar al-Yaum*, 18 August 1956.

30. See Beirut newspapers *al-Kifah al-'Arabi*, *al-Hayat*, and *al-Siyasah*, 7 March 1958, which indicated that the Egyptian Petroleum Workers' Federation had withdrawn from the IFPW at the request of the Syrian Federation of Oil Workers.

31. IFPW, *Union Builder*, 58–5 (October 1958). The IFPW's representative, Curtis J. Hogan, toured the area in 1958 and was scheduled to make another tour in 1959.

32. Government of Iraq, Ministry of Economy, Principal Bureau of Statistics, *Statistical Abstract 1955* (Baghdad, 1956). These figures excluded the retail and wholesale establishments and transportation, which were being covered in two other censuses. The service and petroleum industries were also handled separately.

33. Government of Iraq, *Report on the Census of Services and Service Industries in Iraq for 1957*, *loc. cit.* This was also the first of its kind in Iraq, and included hotels, cinemas, banks, laundries, coffee shops, etc. (The census brought out the importance of coffee shops in Arab life: there were 5534 coffee shops employing 10,445 persons.)

34. Government of Iraq, *Statistical Abstract*, *loc. cit.*, which indicated that 860 of the 15,328 petroleum workers in 1955 were foreigners. The other figures for the railway and port employees were drawn from Lord Salter, *The Development of Iraq: A Plan of Action*, Iraq Development Board (London, 1955), p. 158.

35. See Mahmud M. Habib, "The Labor Movement in Iraq," *Middle Eastern Affairs*, 7.4:137–143 (April 1956); and G. L. Harris, *Iraq: Its People, its Society, its Culture* (Human Relations Area Files: New Haven, 1958), for brief accounts of the labor movement prior to the revolution.

36. International Labour Conference, *Provisional Record*, *op. cit.*, p. 487. In a heated discussion during the International Labour Conference in Geneva in June of 1958, the French delegate rebutted the Iraqi government adviser relative to French suppression of labor in Algeria: "If Mr. Jawad came to the rostrum on behalf of his Government to call for observance of trade union freedoms in Algeria, or in any other country for that matter, then I would say that Mr. Jawad and his Government must have a singular audacity to undertake an exercise of that kind from this rostrum."

37. *Ibid.*

38. 'Aziz Sharif, "Iraq: Building a New Life," *International Affairs*, 5.4:101 f. (Moscow, April 1959).

39. See ICATU, *al-'Ummal al-'Arab,* No. 4 (July 1958), in which several articles on Iraq and the Iraqi labor movement appeared.

40. Beirut *Daily Star*, 3 September 1958. The Iraqi ministers of National Economy and of Social Affairs, Ibrahim Kubbah and Brigadier Naji Talib, who visited Damascus in the first week of September, received representatives of the Confederation of Trade Unions in Syria. Its secretary general, Khalid al-Hakim, expressed hope that Iraqi workers might now be allowed to form trade unions.

41. Cairo newspapers *al-Jumhuriyah*, 17 March 1959; *Akhbar al-Yaum*, 21 March and 4 April 1959.

42. *Akhbar al-Yaum*, 25 April 1959.

43. *Radio Cairo,* 27 April 1959. 'Imad al-'Aziz, one of the pro-Nasir Iraqi labor leaders, attended the ICATU's second congress.

44. *The Iraq Times*, 11 May 1959.

45. Cf. Beling, *loc. cit.*

46. Government of Bahrain, *Census 1950* (Bahrain, 1950).

47. A Bahraini subject was defined in the census as a person born in Bahrain or holding a Bahrain passport.

48. See F. I. Qubain, "Social Classes and Tensions in Bahrain," *Middle East Journal*, 9.3:269–280 (Summer 1955), relative to the social problems they create.

49. In actual fact, the HEC had given way to the Committee of National Unity. This body enjoyed government sanction but was in general identical to the HEC.

50. *The Bahrain Labour Ordinance, 1957, loc. cit.* (The Arabic text is the official text.)

51. Government of Bahrain, *Annual Report for Year 1956, loc. cit.*; and Hazard, *loc. cit.*

52. *1957 Report of Operations to the Saudi Arab Government by the Arabian American Oil Company*, 1958.

53. Kingdom of Saudi Arabia, Ministry of Finance, *Compensation Regulations for Workmen in Technical Industrial Enterprises*, Approved by High Decree No. 8/4/4 dated 18/7/1356 (23 September 1937), (2nd ed.; in Arabic; Mecca: Government Press, 1363 [1943–44]).

54. Kingdom of Saudi Arabia, Ministry of Finance, *Labor and Workman Regulations*, Approved by High Decree issued on 25/11/1366 (10 October 1947), (in Arabic; Mecca: Government Press, 1367 [1947–48]).

55. Royal Decree No. 17/2/23/2639, *loc. cit.*

56. These committees are like the early employee representation plans in the U.S.A. Generally speaking, the committees are supposed to confine their attention to matters affecting employee relations, such as recreation, living accommodations, work rules, safety, etc. Normally the committees do not discuss wages, money emoluments, vacations, benefits or terms of employment. The Iraq Petroleum Company (IPC) introduced joint consultative committees into its operation in Iraq a number of years ago. The

trade unions, however, opposed their establishment in the IPC operations in Syria.

57. *Annual Report of the Department of Social Affairs, 1957, loc. cit.*

58. There are a number of clubs, however, which apparently perform some of the functions of trade unions.

59. In addition, representatives of other international trade union organizations have also been kept out. Curtis Hogan of the ICFTU, for example, was able to get as near as Bahrain but could not get into Arabia twenty miles away.

60. 'Abd al-Mughni Sa'id Salamah, "The Arab Workers in the International Field," *al-Mujtama'*, 1.2,3:4 ff. (April/May, 1958). In essence, the same article appeared a little later in the ICATU's official organ (*al-'Ummal al-'Arab*, no. 4 [July 1958]). This is indicative of the close tie-up between the ICATU and the nascent labor movement in Kuwait.

61. *Aden, Revised Edition of the Laws, 1955, Subsidiary Legislation*, Chap. 152, "Trade Unions and Trade Disputes" (London, 1955), which provides the legal basis for the present movement.

62. See Aden Colony, Department of Labour and Welfare, *Annual Report, 1955* and *Annual Report, 1956–1957* (Aden: Government Printer, n.d.). Five other organizations were listed as trade unions, but they were actually employer associations. The ICFTU *Report of the Fifth World Congress, op. cit.*, credited the Aden TUC with having 8945 members in January 1957.

63. From correspondence with the Labor Commissioner in Aden, Mr. C. Spencer-Cooke.

Chapter VI

POSITIVE NEUTRALITY AND ARAB LABOR

1. See L. L. Lorwin, *The International Labor Movement: History, Policies, Outlook* (New York, 1953); J. P. Windmuller, *American Labor and the International Labor Movement: 1940 to 1953*, Cornell International and Labor Relations Reports, No. 2 (Ithaca, 1955), for historical surveys of the rise and development of the WFTU and the ICFTU.

2. The only important national trade union center absent from the WFTU's founding conference was the American Federation of Labor (AFL). It refused to take part in the conference for several reasons, one of which was that it opposed the participation of the Soviet trade unions. The AFL remained outside the WFTU where, in fact, the AFL developed a large international program of its own to oppose Communism. The AFL and the CIO, however, were among the principal founders of the new ICFTU.

3. Lorwin, *op cit.*, pp. 266, 318; U.S. Department of Labor, Office of International Labor Affairs, *Directory of World Federation of Trade Unions (WFTU)* and *Directory of International Confederation of Free Trade Unions (ICFTU)* (1955 and 1956, respectively). The ICFTU's total membership is now around 55 million. Roughly three-fourths of the membership represented at its founding conference were from western Europe and North America. Since then, to the ICFTU's discomfort, the trend has been to increase the Western proportion as the absolute membership grows. About 90 per cent of the WFTU's 90 million members are in the Soviet Union, the "People's Democracies" behind the Iron Curtain, Communist China, and in North Korea. Its headquarters were initially located in Paris, but were then moved to Vienna and finally to Prague.

4. See Zaki Badaoui, *La Législation du Travail au Moyen-Orient* (reprint of article which appeared in the *Journal du Commerce et de la Marine*) (Alexandria, n.d.), pp. 29 ff.; Abdel Raouf Abou Alam, *loc. cit.*; and Stauffer, *loc. cit.*, for partial lists of Arab trade unionists attending the early congresses of the WFTU and the ICFTU.

5. L. L. Lorwin, "The Structure of International Labor Activities," *The Annals of the American Academy of Political and Social Science*, 310: 1–11 (March 1957).

6. Nevertheless, the ITF still carries the Egyptian organizations on its membership roles, along with affiliates in the Sudan and Tunisia in the Arab world. (*International Transport Workers' Journal*, 19.4 [April 1959].)

7. For convenience sake, the ICFTU has grouped the Aden TUC with African affiliates in some instances (e.g., relative to trade union leadership courses in the trade union college at Kampala, Uganda).

8. ICFTU, *Report of the Fifth World Congress, op. cit.*

9. ICFTU, *The ICFTU and the Workers of Morocco, op. cit.*

10. Cf. the official organ of the ICFTU, *Free Labour World*, *passim*, and the ICFTU, *Report of the Fifth World Congress, op. cit.*

11. *Ibid.*

12. See Arnold Beichman, "Trade Unions in the Middle East," *Commentary*, 22:276 f. (September 1956), for a brief account of the situation just as Morocco and Tunisia had attained their independence.

13. ICFTU, *Report of the Fifth World Congress, op. cit.*, p. 104, relative to the ICFTU's protest against the Saudi anti-strike decree.

14. In particular they object to the movements in the UAR. These, they insist, are not "free" trade unions but are vehicles created for other purposes than trade unionism.

15. Lorwin, *The International Labor Movement, op. cit.*, pp. 277 ff.

16. ICFTU, *Report of the Second World Congress* (Brussels, 1952).

17. ICFTU, *Report of the Fifth World Congress, op. cit.*

18. *Ibid.*, pp. 350 ff.

19. *Ibid.*, pp. 183 ff. Membership figures were reported to the ICFTU for 1 January 1957, as follows: Israel's Histadrut — 579,335; Lebanon's *Ligue*

des Syndicats — 15,327; and Aden's TUC — 8,945. To be sure, there are large Arab labor movements outside the ICFTU's Middle East area; e.g., Morocco's UMT, Tunisia's UGTT, and Egypt's ECL.

20. It was one of the reasons given, however, for the withdrawal of the Egyptian Federation of Petroleum and Chemical Workers from the International Federation of Petroleum Workers.

21. The Latin American labor organizations: the *Confederación de Trabajadores de America Latina* (CTAL) affiliated with the WFTU, and the *Organización Regional Interamericana de Trabajadores* (ORIT), the regional organization of the ICFTU, are cases in point.

22. *Al-Jumhuriyah*, 4 April 1956.

23. ICATU, *al-'Ummal al-'Arab*, *op. cit.*, *passim.*

24. There was a sharp exchange of letters between the ICFTU and the ICATU in 1958. The quoted portions have been drawn from a letter from Fathi Kamil of the ICATU, dated 14 May 1958. The correspondence was reproduced and distributed by the ICFTU.

25. ICATU, *al-'Ummal al-'Arab*, no. 1 (November 1958), pp. 21–23. There were two observers listed officially from the Egyptian Trade Union Congress at the Accra conference. In his report, however, the ICATU's secretary general indicated that these same representatives functioned as its unofficial observers at the conference.

26. ICFTU, *Report of the Fifth World Congress*, *op. cit.*

27. *Ibid.* With reference to the political aims of the ICATU, Ahmad Talili of the UGTT asked, "But what organization does not go in for politics?" The UMT's al-Mahjub ibn al-Sadiq protested against the "gratuitous attack on the Arab Federation of Labor." The charge that the ICATU was anti-Israel, of course, failed to arouse any antipathy towards the ICATU among the Arab delegates. In fact, if anything it had the opposite effect.

28. *Ibid.* In fact, the Lebanese delegation had submitted a formal resolution calling for a clearly defined position towards the pan-Arab confederation, which the Lebanese delegation characterized as being "guided above all by a political aim. . . ."

29. Mahmud al-'Ajami and 'Abd al-Mun'im al-Ghazali, *The ICFTU's Plots Against African and Arab Workers*, Published by the Office of Labor Propaganda and Education (in Arabic: Cairo, n.d.). When the ICFTU objected to this book, the ICATU pointed out that this was not its publication.

30. See correspondence referred to earlier between the secretaries general of the ICATU and the ICFTU. Fathi Kamil summarized the ICATU's position by stating that the "Eastern comrades are fully supporting us in our aims . . . ."

Chapter VII

COMMUNISM AND THE PAN-ARAB LABOR MOVEMENT

1. Bernard Lewis, "The Middle Eastern Reaction to Soviet Pressures," *Middle East Journal*, 10.2:125–137 (Spring 1956), refers to this lack of experience with Russian imperialism, and also points out the consequent double standard applied in the Middle East to Western and Soviet actions. Gift horses from the West, for example, are given dental x-rays and rejected, or accepted grudgingly as if they were part-payment of a debt. Mere Soviet promises, however, are accepted with wild acclaim.

2. Walter Z. Laqueur, "The Appeal of Communism in the Middle East," *Middle East Journal*, 9.1:17–27 (Winter 1955).

3. E.g., the present Egyptian regime has taken a lively interest in both the industrial workers and the peasants. Indicative of the latter is the recent statement of President 'Abd al-Nasir: "Our most urgent need is to introduce social and economic progress, and then we will have a suitable democratic system. We are now seeking to develop a form of democracy suited to our conditions. We will widen the basis of our National Union Party and base it on agricultural cooperatives, through elections in every village and rural center . . ." (*Radio Cairo* and *Radio Voice of the Arabs*, 18 April 1959). Similar interest in the peasants has been recently generated in Iraq.

4. Walter Z. Laqueur, "Communism in Jordan," *The World Today*, 12.3:110 f. (March 1956); and Martin Ebon, *World Communism Today* (New York, 1948), p. 413.

5. M. Perlmann, "Labor in Syria and Lebanon," *Palestine Affairs*, 3.6:75 f. (June 1948).

6. Bakdash, *loc. cit.*

7. See the WFTU's official monthly organ, *World Trade Union Movement*, *passim*; and S. A. Dange, *Trade Union Tasks in the Fight against Colonialism*, Report presented to the Fourth World Trade Union Congress, Leipzig, October 4–15, 1957 (London, n.d.), *passim*, relative to the action taken by the WFTU in support of the workers in the Arab world.

8. *Fédération Syndicale des Ouvriers et Employés du Liban.* Its membership is estimated at about 2400. The federation has refused to register with the government, as required by law.

9. U.S. Department of Labor, Bureau of Labor Statistics, *Summary of the Labor Situation in Lebanon*, *op. cit.*

10. The Republic of the Sudan, Ministry of Social Affairs, Labour Department, *Report covering the Period, 1st July 1953 — 30th June, 1955* (Sudan, n.d.), p. 2.

11. G. E. Lichtblau, "The World Federation of Trade Unions," *Social Research* (Spring 1958), pp. 1–36.

12. Official WFTU organ, *World Trade Union Movement*, No. 10 (October 1956); *ibid.* No. 9 (September 1957). Both list Ibrahim Bakri, secretary of the Mechanical Weavers' Federation of Syria, as a member of the WFTU's executive council. He was the Syrian delegate to the WFTU's founding conference in Paris in 1945.

13. *Ibid.*, No. 4 (April 1959), pp. 40f.

14. *Ibid.*

15. *N. Y. Times*, 2 May 1959.

16. *Radio Baghdad*, 26 April 1959. The Iraqi council of ministers, it appears, reached this decision on April 24, the day on which the ICATU's second congress was scheduled to commence in Cairo. Arab Labor Day, according to the ICATU, falls on 24 March — the anniversary date of the ICATU.

17. *Al-Jumhuriyah*, 17 March 1959; weekly *Akhbar al-Yaum*, 21 March 1959; WFTU, *World Trade Union Movement*, No. 4 (April 1959). Conflicting labor organizations apparently were in the same fields. It appears, however, that the Communist unions had received government licenses to operate while the others had not.

18. WFTU, *World Trade Union Movement*, No. 11 (November 1957), pp. 54 ff., and Special Number (July 1956); *Texts and Decision of the Fourth World Trade Union Congress* (London, n.d.).

19. ICATU, *Constitution*, *op. cit.*, Article 6, Sec. 15.

20. U.S. Dept. of Labor, *Directories*, *op. cit.*; Donahue, *op. cit.*

21. Al-'Ajami and al-Ghazali, *op. cit.*, p. 57.

22. See ICATU, *al-'Ummal al-'Arab*, No. 2 (January 1958), for the texts of the joint communiqués with organized labor in China, Indonesia, Japan, and Morocco.

23. National Bank of Egypt (SAE), *Economic Bulletin*, 10.4:375 (Cairo, 1957). In addition, the permanent secretariat of the Afro-Asian Solidarity Council in Cairo was given the following instructions: "The Conference requests its permanent Cairo Bureau to establish the widest possible contact with the trade unions and cooperative organizations in Asia and Africa in order to promote cooperation for the realization of the above-mentioned purposes."

24. H. A. Jack, "The Cairo Conference," *Africa Today*, 5.2:3–9 (March–April 1958). In fact Dr. Jack links the Afro-Asian Solidarity Conference directly to the pro-Communist World Peace Council held in Stockholm in 1954.

25. *N. Y. Times*, 9 December 1958. Indonesia opposed the USSR's participation in the Afro-Asian Economic Conference held in Cairo on the grounds that the USSR was neither Asian nor African.

26. See WFTU *World Trade Union Movement*, No. 11 (November 1958); and ICATU *al-'Ummal al-'Arab*, No. 5 (October 1958), for accounts of the conference and the background.

27. I. Bakri, "Arab Trade Unions Draw Close Together," *World Trade Union Movement*, No. 10 (October 1956).

28. Walter Z. Laqueur, "The Prospects of Communism in the Middle East," *Tensions in the Middle East*, ed. Philip W. Thayer (Baltimore, 1958), pp. 297–314.

29. E.g., the ICATU made public declarations of solidarity with the WFTU in its aims and programs. Then at the ILO conference in Geneva in June 1957, the ICATU reportedly refused to go along with a motion to condemn Russian suppression of Hungarian liberties, on the ground that "this position was clearly the carrying out of America's imperialistic policy." Cf. al-'Ajami and al-Ghazali, *op. cit.*, p. 58. (It is of interest to note that in the wake of Communism's imperialistic inroads in the Near East, Cairo's *Akhbar al-Yaum* published a book in the spring of 1959 on the Hungarian revolution and the subsequent Communist terror and despotism. The entire publication was reportedly sold out in a week.)

30. WFTU, *World Trade Union Movement*, Nos. 8–9 (August/September 1958).

31. *Ibid.*

32. See Cairo weekly *Akhbar al-Yaum*, 8 March 1958, editorial, which criticizes the ICATU on this point.

Chapter VIII

PROBLEMS AND PROSPECTS OF THE PAN-ARAB LABOR MOVEMENT

1. G. C. Lodge, "Labor's Role in Newly Developing Countries," *Foreign Affairs*, 37.4:660–671 (July 1959).

2. Harbison, *loc. cit.* Cf. J. S. Badeau, "The Middle East: Conflict in Priorities," "*Foreign Affairs*, 36.2:240 (January 1958), for a similar opinion: "I believe that in the perspective of history the Egyptian revolution will be to the Middle East what the French Revolution was to Europe. It, too, had its self-seeking leaders, its power cliques, its political nationalism; but it let loose forces that finally changed the pattern of social life in most of Europe. That is what the Egyptian revolution has begun to do in the Middle East and that is why it strikes fire in some form in every country."

3. Albert Hourani, "The Middle East and the Crisis of 1956," *Middle Eastern Affairs, Number One*, St. Antony's Papers, No. 4 (London, 1958), pp. 9–42.